NEURODIVERSITY
AND EDUCATION

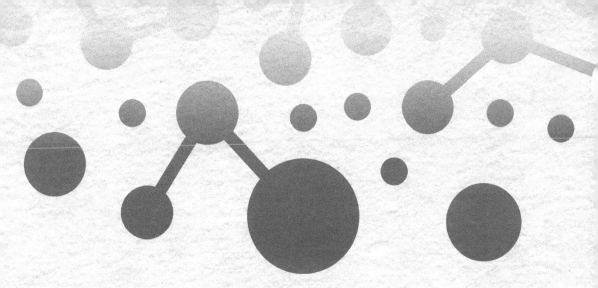

PAUL ELLIS
AMANDA KIRBY
ABBY OSBORNE

NEURODIVERSITY AND EDUCATION

CORWIN

A SAGE company
2455 Teller Road
Thousand Oaks, California 91320
(0800)233-9936
www.corwin.com

SAGE Publications Ltd
1 Oliver's Yard
55 City Road
London EC1Y 1SP

SAGE Publications India Pvt Ltd
B 1/I 1 Mohan Cooperative Industrial Area
Mathura Road
New Delhi 110 044

SAGE Publications Asia-Pacific Pte Ltd
3 Church Street
#10-04 Samsung Hub
Singapore 049483

Editor: Amy Thornton
Senior project editor: Chris Marke
Marketing manager: Dilhara Attygalle
Cover design: Wendy Scott
Typeset by: C&M Digitals (P) Ltd, Chennai, India

Library of Congress Control Number: 2022945313

British Library Cataloguing in Publication Data

A catalogue record for this book is available from the British Library.

ISBN 978-1-5296-0036-0
ISBN 978-1-5296-0035-3 (pbk)

At SAGE we take sustainability seriously. Most of our products are printed in the UK using responsibly sourced papers and boards. When we print overseas we ensure sustainable papers are used as measured by the PREPS grading system. We undertake an annual audit to monitor our sustainability.

CONTENTS

LIST OF FIGURES AND TABLES

FIGURES

TABLES

DEDICATION

This book is dedicated to anyone who has ever been denied the opportunity to learn because they do not conform to the norm, and to all those who share the goal of making education more neuro-inclusive.

ABOUT THE AUTHORS

Paul Ellis began teaching in schools and universities in the 1990s and has held senior positions in two of the main global education providers – the International Baccalaureate and Cambridge University Press & Assessment – since 2006. He has worked with teachers and school leaders on all continents as a workshop leader and conference presenter, and to advise and support schools in their professional learning needs. He broadcasts regularly on educational topics and has written or edited more than a dozen education books, including *The Trainer Toolkit* and *The What, Why and How of Assessment*, also published by Corwin.

Professor Amanda Kirby has an international reputation and is a recognised authority in the field of neurodiversity, having extensive personal and professional experience in the area. She is an emeritus professor at the University of South Wales and an honorary professor at Cardiff University, and founded and ran a transdisciplinary clinical and research team relating to neurodiversity for 20 years. She has a PhD related to neurodiversity. Amanda is the founder and CEO of Do-IT Solutions, a tech-for-good company, and currently chairs the ADHD Foundation. She is also co-author with Theo Smith of *Neurodiversity at Work: Drive Innovation, Performance and Productivity with a Neurodiverse Workforce* which won the UK Business Book Awards in 2022.

Abby Osborne has extensive experience in training teachers in inclusive curriculum design. She also has a background in mentoring and tutoring neurodivergent students in secondary, further and higher education. Abby currently works at the University of Bath's Centre for Teaching and Learning supporting colleagues to implement inclusive teaching and learning practices. Abby also works as an educational consultant, most recently working with Cambridge Assessment International Education to develop guidance and training materials for international teachers about inclusive education.

INTRODUCTION

The 21st century and the digital age have given us the freedom, the tools and the potential to make our world a place where all are welcome to be who they are and who they can become. In many areas of life, we are now much more willing and able to talk and work with equity and diversity in mind – and to take positive action for inclusivity and belonging. Many countries, companies and organisations have introduced laws, policies and roles to underline and promote their commitment to such action and, consequently, many more people can thrive for the collective benefit of humanity.

But there is still a lot more to be done – both in the workplace and, most importantly, in education. Awareness of the importance of equity, diversity, inclusivity and belonging has benefitted some sections of society but has stopped short, so far, for others. Despite an increased focus on key areas such as ethnicity, gender and sexuality, far less has been discussed – and celebrated – about our *cognitive* differences, also known as our **neurodiversity**. We are thus neglecting the potential of a vast number of people and denying them the opportunity to shine.

A spotlight on neurodiversity can help us explore questions such as:

- What is it about our brains that make each of us see, hear, speak, act, move and think in unique ways?
- How do the context and the environment we are placed in and our interactions with others shape our ability to thrive?
- What can we do to support ourselves and each other to navigate a world that is often uniform, standardised and designed for a mythical average person?

Our goal in writing this book is to show that neurodiversity is about us all and the variations we have in our cognitive functioning. Neurodiversity is not an exclusive club or one condition, difficulty, difference, or disorder: it is about every one of us. Understanding more about the concept of neuro-diversity can help us consider, respect and appreciate these differences – and see potential rather than deficits in ourselves and in each other.

In simple terms, we want to help you know more about the barriers – or interferences – that prevent individuals from flourishing, and what we can do to remove them. The value of spotting what is getting in the way of someone fulfilling their potential, and doing something about it, can be summed up in a simple formula first suggested some 50 years ago by the former interna-tional tennis player turned sports and business coach, Tim Gallwey:

Performance = potential *minus* interference

Interferences may result from other people and their interactions with us – such as how they speak or listen to us or enable us to contribute to an activity; the environments in which we live, work and play – which may not have been designed with inclusivity in mind; and the pathways that we feel obliged to follow to achieve recognised success. Interferences can also result from our own motivations or the ways in which we approach the world around us. We may not even see the barriers that exist because we encounter them on a daily basis, and they have been generally accepted as the norm.

How we prepare ourselves to deal with interferences begins in our early development and throughout our education as children and young adults. How we learn and what we do with our learning can make a big difference to our resilience and to our dependency on others later in our lives.

In this book we aim to tell you more about neurodiversity and give you some practical ideas and tools to use in your own context so that more of us can access, participate and make progress through evidence-informed, high-quality and well-designed education programmes. In so-doing, we echo – and, by emphasising the value to society of *embracing* inclusivity, go beyond – the words of the Right Honourable Helen Clark, Chair of the Global Education

Monitoring Report Advisory Board, in her introduction to UNESCO's 2020 issue, *Inclusion in Education: All Means All*:

> education systems are only as inclusive as their creators make them. Disadvantage can be created by these systems and their contexts. It exists where people's needs are not taken into account. Inclusion in education is about ensuring that every learner feels valued and respected, and can enjoy a clear sense of belonging. [...] [M]any changes can be made for free, in gestures made by teachers, in the ethos school leaders create for their learning environments, in the way families make decisions when school choices are presented to them, and in what we, as a society, decide we want for our future.
>
> (p. 8)

This book is for educators, or those with an interest in education. It is for teachers, school leaders, college principals, researchers and policy-makers, in whichever country you live and at whatever stage you are in your career. We want you to see this book as part of your ongoing professional commitment to give young people the best start in life so they can play, study and thrive with as little interference as possible.

We have written this book with the benefit of our own experiences and expertise as researchers and practitioners, and as advocates and allies for neurodivergence. We have all been teachers and leaders in education and we have included what we think is most useful for educators to know.

You are welcome to read the book in the order that you prefer but, as we often refer in later chapters to what has come before, you may benefit from working through each chapter in turn. To help you navigate, we start and end each chapter with a summary of what it contains. We have also included at the end of the book, arranged by chapter, a selection of resources for further reading, viewing or listening. We have done our best to acknowledge our sources but encourage you to contact our publishers if you think we have missed or misrepresented any ideas contained in the book.

In the **first three chapters** we describe what neurodiversity is and the other terms associated with it, such as special educational needs and specific diagnoses. We also give a historical perspective on how those with neurodivergent conditions have been categorised and treated, and how this has led to inequality and inequity in some aspects of education and society. In **Chapter 4** we discuss mental health and wellbeing and how the ways in which we all feel and function can be closely associated with the ways our brains and bodies work and our interactions with our environment and other people.

In **Chapters 5 and 6** we then consider how we could re-evaluate the ways we think about 'special' educational needs so that we become more inclusive in our approach, and design educational opportunities with this in mind. This leads onto **Chapters 7 and 8**, where we talk in practical terms about how we can teach so that all students learn better, and to **Chapter 9**, where we look at the ways we assess young people both summatively and formatively, and how we might also make testing fairer and more accessible. Our focus for the **final chapter** is on what we can also do to make the education workplace more inclusive, not only for students but also for teachers, school leaders and parents.

We hope that you will enjoy the book for its content and for the contribution it makes to the growing argument to recognise and celebrate that we share – and all have so much to gain from – a world that is neurodiverse. Above all, we would like you to join us in doing all that you can as a result of what you read in this book to promote inclusivity and belonging in your daily interactions with people and the world around you, through education and beyond.

1

WHAT IS NEURODIVERSITY?

In this chapter we will consider:

- the current understanding of the language relating to neurodiversity;
- the concept of neurodiversity and what this means in the context of education;
- how we are moving from a condition-specific approach to a person-centred approach, which captures strengths as well as challenges;
- how we, and our environment, can change over time, and the impact this has on our functioning.

WHAT IS NEURODIVERSITY?

Neurodiversity describes the different ways that we all think, move, hear, see, understand, process information and communicate with each other. We are all neurodiverse. We each have an amazing 86 billion brain cells connected in billions of different ways.

The word 'neurodiversity' is credited to Australian sociologist Judy Singer and the US journalist Harvey Blume who were both using it at around the same time in the late 1990s. Blume described neurodiversity as: 'being as crucial for humans as biodiversity is for life in general'. Every ecosystem contains a unique collection of species (humans being one of them), all interacting with each other and specifically surviving in that setting. In the same way that we consider plants, animals and reptiles, we can consider humans and how we have adapted over time to succeed and survive in specific settings. Therefore, we all have our place in the world.

The current education ecosystem not only doesn't fit all students but also doesn't encourage those with certain traits. This means we can all miss out and not benefit from the potential that exists and can result from such diversity. What we have in some ways is a mismatch between where education is and what it values, and evolution having maintained some specific and useful neurodivergent traits. These traits have been retained as a part of natural selection and in the 21st century, if they are recognised and harnessed, they can be extremely useful for society.

UNPACKING NEURODIVERSITY

As we have identified, neurodiversity is not a narrow concept relating to one condition or one area of cognition. However, for many years researchers hunted for specific genes to try to understand and locate the underlying mechanisms for a specific condition such as dyslexia, so that they would know how to support students.

It was believed that if we knew what the underlying 'cause' was, then we could seek a cure for 'the condition'. The approach was very much grounded in a *deficit* model with the aim of fixing 'faulty' brains rather than seeing the variation in society that actually exists. In recent times there has also been a backlash from those with lived experience of autism spectrum conditions (ASC) who have expressed some concerns that gene studies could lead us towards eugenics and potentially deleting what may be seen as 'faulty' genes.

We will explain later about the different conditions often considered under the umbrella of neurodiversity (see Figure 1.1). These days we talk far more about spectra of conditions and seeing neurodiversity as multidimensional instead of focusing on one specific condition in isolation and as a narrow categorisation.

Extensive research into conditions such as attention deficit hyperactivity disorder (ADHD) and ASC in the last few years has shown that while there are in fact many genes relating to each condition there are also many genes that influence both conditions. The concept of neurodiversity embraces this understanding. Appreciating the concept of co-occurrence is important because it goes to the heart of understanding each student and not delivering support according to one diagnosis or another. The reality is that while gene studies may lead us to a greater understanding of the underlying mechanisms of actions, it is far more complex than a simple linear relation between the genes and behaviours we see. The environment you are in, now or in the past, can also react with genes and shape our experiences and alter outcomes at all stages of our life.

The neurodiversity paradigm moves us away from the 'good brain/bad brain' narrative and embraces the understanding that autism spectrum conditions – and other conditions – represent a necessary part of human diversity. These differences continue to be present in humans because traits confer some advantage regarding natural selection.

The increasing value placed on understanding the environment is important for educational professionals as it means we need to consider the past and present ecosystem of the student when planning support. In **Chapter 3** we will look at what happens when we do not consider the ecosystems and the individual's potential and how this can result in some students being missed, misdiagnosed or misunderstood.

Teachers have a crucial part to play in shaping success for every student by creating a more inclusive world, and can either encourage participation in our society or create barriers or interferences to growth and success. Understanding the link between the student and their environment is fundamental to achieving greater success.

WHAT TERMS ARE ASSOCIATED WITH NEURODIVERSITY?

Neurodiversity is still a relatively new word for many people, so terms associated with it and their usage are still evolving. Figure 1.1 shows a selection of the terms that some people are beginning to use that you may find useful. This figure shows a bell curve with neurodivergent traits positively skewed to the right and neurodivergent challenges skewed to the left.

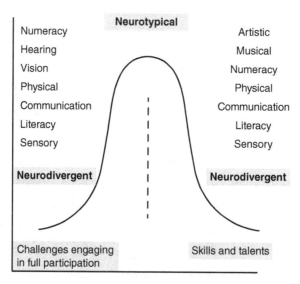

Figure 1.1   Bell curve showing strong skills and challenges

DEVELOPMENTAL AND ACQUIRED NEURODIVERSITY

When we talk about neurodivergent traits there are some conditions that we usually consider under this umbrella term. These conditions or traits may either be *developmental* (born with) and/or *acquired* through child and adulthood. People can be both born with traits that diverge from the typical presentation and/or acquire other challenges later in life because of trauma or developing a specific condition affecting their cognition. Someone could also be born with dyslexia and, for example, develop Parkinsonism as well later in their life.

NEUROTYPICAL

'Neurotypical' is a term used when someone fits within the socially and culturally defined cognitive norm. What is deemed neurotypical in one setting, location or context may not be in another. The way children are parented for example varies globally and this may result in differences in child development rates such as the age of walking. When we ignore cultural variation and consider development only from a Western perspective, we may create 'blind spots' in our understanding of child development.

As an example, the Pirahã indigenous people of the Amazon rainforest are cognitively able but anumeric (i.e., don't count). This is very unusual, as only a small portion of the world's languages are anumeric or nearly anumeric. But this is one example that demonstrates that having the terms and skills to associate items with numbers is not universal to human beings. When people do not have number words, they struggle to make quantitative distinctions that probably seem natural to those who use maths in everyday life.

NEURODIVERGENT

The term 'neurodivergent' refers to someone diverging from the average or socially derived norm (see Figure 1.1). If we consider the different cognitive elements such as our ability to spell, read, move and understand, we can *positively* diverge if we have strengths in specific areas, such as being very good at maths, and *negatively* diverge if, for example, we have challenges with literacy skills such as those associated with dyslexia.

SPIKY PROFILES

Each of us will have different 'spiky' profiles (see Figure 1.2). Our spikes represent our strengths. Nobody is 'good' or 'bad' at everything but some of

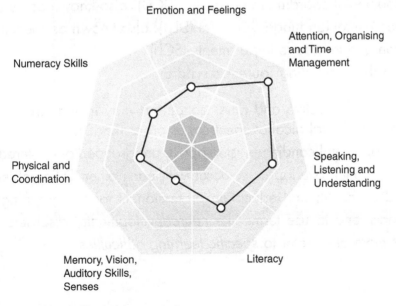

Figure 1.2   Spiky profile (Kirby, 2022)

us will have 'spikier' profiles where there are greater differences between and among our skills and challenges that impact on our day-to-day functioning. We may also have exceptional or hidden skills in some areas that we cannot showcase unless we are given an opportunity to do so. When we can understand our strengths and know how to use these to the maximum, we can offset some of the challenges we experience. When we do this effectively our strengths are often in the areas that we end up focusing on for our careers.

DEVELOPMENTAL CONDITIONS

Developmental conditions are generally categorised using two international classification systems organised by the World Health Organization (WHO) and American Psychiatric Association (APA). They describe each neurodevelopmental condition using a set of behavioural characteristics.

Developmental conditions may include:

- attention deficit hyperactivity disorder (ADHD), including attention deficit disorder (ADD)
- autism spectrum conditions or disorder (ASC/ASD)
- dyslexia
- dyscalculia
- developmental coordination disorder (DCD), also known as dyspraxia
- developmental language disorders (DLD), also known as speech, communication and language impairments (SCLI)
- tic disorders (including Tourette's syndrome).

This list is not exhaustive and other conditions may include traumatic brain injury (TBI) and foetal alcohol spectrum disorder (FASD).

The developmental conditions listed above are grouped or clustered together because they often overlap or co-occur with each other. Different terms have been used by health and education professionals for the groupings. Health professionals tend to use terms like *neurodevelopmental disorders*, whereas educators more often refer to *specific learning difficulties*.

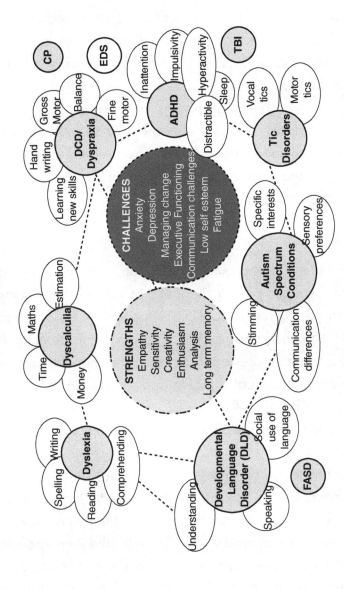

Figure 1.3 Different conditions commonly associated with neurodiversity

Note: ADHD – attention deficit hyperactivity disorder; CP – cerebral palsy; FASD – foetal alcohol spectrum disorder; DLD – developmental language disorder; TBI – traumatic brain injury.

One problem with the groupings is there is not only a lack of consistency in definition for each term and conditions included in each grouping but the definitions may differ by professional grouping as well. For example, dyspraxia, also known as developmental coordination disorder (DCD), can sometimes be seen as an 'educational' condition and included in the group 'specific learning difficulties' whereas in fact it is defined in the American Psychiatric Association categorisation system DSM-5 as a medical condition. Inconsistent terminology can lead to confusion for parents trying to navigate health and educational systems as well as for educators when trying to ensure their students thrive.

Figure 1.3 shows an example of groupings we often associate with some common neurodivergent traits. The central two circles show common themes of both strengths and challenges that may co-occur with different conditions. The circles at the edges show the clustering of certain characteristics that are related to each specific condition.

ACQUIRED CONDITIONS

Today we recognise that throughout our lives our brains can change – especially in later adolescence. Synaptic pruning happens as part of the developmental process in these teen years and is especially important in the development of more mature organisation and planning skills. During synaptic pruning, the brain eliminates extra synapses. Synapses are brain structures that allows the neurons to transmit an electrical or chemical signal to another neuron. We explore this in some more detail in **Chapter 4**.

As we mentioned above, we may also acquire new cognitive conditions during our lifetime, such as Parkinson's disease. Here, neurons that produce the neurotransmitter dopamine die off in the basal ganglia, an area of the brain that controls body movements. This causes difficulty initiating movements and can also alter the way that someone processes information and communicates.

Other conditions can be acquired either through inheriting specific genes (such as Huntingdon's disease) associated with the condition, or through environmental challenges such as having a head injury. This can also result in an alteration of the way you process information, think, act and move. Other examples are:

- multiple sclerosis (MS)
- traumatic brain injury (TBI)
- cerebrovascular accident (CVA), also known as a stroke
- brain tumours.

NEUROMINORITY

A neurominority is defined as a distinct group or groups of people who diverge from a social norm. The term has been associated with people with conditions such as ASC, ADHD, dyslexia, DCD, DLD and tic disorders. Some people, because they are defined as belonging to a group differing from others, can feel a sense of separation and exclusion from participation and feel more marginalised by the society they live in.

Recognising you belong to a specific minority can, however, help you reframe yourself in a positive way and be a means of finding others who are having similar life experiences and have a shared understanding. Some campaigners describe themselves as being a part of a 'neurodiversity move-ment', recognising they have a condition or conditions in common with others so that they can better advocate for themselves.

UNDERSTANDING OF NEURODIVERSITY VARIES ACROSS COUNTRIES

The government and laws of a specific country can either open or close access to identification, support, recognition and services for those who are neurodivergent. This may be related to the way categorisation of need is defined. In England, for example, laws such as the Autism Act (2009) have been passed and enforce the delivery of specific actions and services for those individuals who have gained a diagnosis of autism.

This may be helpful for some but not for all. While awareness has increased especially in relationship to autism, the approach of singling out and favouring one specific condition over others may indirectly result in further inequity.

The reason for focusing on one specific condition more than others may result from lack of recognition of overlap, lack of services, or lack of knowledge by professionals of these other conditions. Individuals may have the same level of challenge in accessing education and participating in society as those with autism but may have the 'wrong' diagnosis, in terms of what currently attracts funding and support. Today we are increasingly recognising that the different developmental conditions overlap and why we need to move from a narrow 'condition-specific' approach to understanding the pattern and needs of each student.

MOVING FROM DEFICIT TO DISCOVERING STRENGTHS

Until relatively recently our view of students with learning differences has tended to focus more on negatives, with a diagnosis usually based on emphasising these. Furthermore, a diagnosis only provides a snapshot of ability in a moment in time and does not capture what a learner may be capable of in the future or with the right support, or how they have performed in the past in a different setting.

We describe conditions with terms such as *dys*-lexia meaning difficulties with reading, or attention *deficit* hyperactivity *disorder*. When people see themselves defined in terms of what they can't do, it can have a long-term impact on their sense of self. They can feel different from others around them and have a sense of shame, low self-esteem and lack self-confidence. These feelings can remain with that person throughout their life. There is extensive evidence across the field of neurodiversity of increased rates of mental health challenges and lowered self-esteem compared to those who travel through education and life with ease. We will explore this more in detail in **Chapter 4**.

Excitingly, more recently we have begun to consider how the positive skills associated with neurodivergent profiles can bring advantages to the individual and society. This echoes Blume's thoughts on how crucial neurodiversity is for society. Some people with dyslexia, for example, have been noted for their visual thinking ability and entrepreneurial strengths. Some people with ADHD can thrive where they can use their skills in developing novel solutions to complex problems. People with ADHD may also be more inclined to take calculated risks and be more entrepreneurial. Some individuals with autism spectrum traits have good analytical skills relating to computer programming or mathematical computation. Some people even talk about 'superpowers' associated with neurodivergent thinkers.

We should not overplay this, however. While essential to seek out strengths in each person, we must also be careful not to create stereotypes such as assuming that all autistic people are good at IT or mathematics, or that all dyslexic people are creative. We cannot attribute a set of thinking approaches to a single label because each person will be different. Additionally, we mustn't forget that some students will continue to face huge barriers to accessing education because of, for example, physical or linguistic challenges and some students may need high levels of day-to-day support. While we are not saying that every neurodivergent individual will go on to be a genius, it is important that we get better at identifying interference in all its forms so that each learner fulfils their potential.

DELIVERING FOR ALL

We have identified the importance of considering the ecosystem in terms of ensuring we better understand, support and harness those who are seen to diverge from present-day social norms. We will talk about this in greater detail in **Chapter 3**. Nowhere is the ecosystem more important than in the education system, yet schools have delivered education predominantly in the same way for more than two centuries. Children are grouped in classes, and the content is often delivered at one pace with a teacher facing the class for set periods of time. It has been designed for an 'average' student and mainly for efficiency. But this approach means that it will favour some students more than others. We sometimes use the metaphor 'fitting a square peg in a round hole' (see Figure 1.4).

Figure 1.4   A square peg in a round hole

If you are a 'round peg'-shaped student – that is, a student who thrives using the dominant modes of teaching and learning – you may glide through school because you fit the shape of current educational provision and expectations. You can engage in lessons, join in with team games and communicate reasonably well with your peers. However, if you are a 'square-shaped' peg, then education may be harder for you to navigate as you may not be able to participate as easily or play team sports well, or stay focused in a lesson for more than ten to 15 minutes.

CHILDREN LEARN AND PROGRESS AT DIFFERENT RATES AND IN DIFFERENT ENVIRONMENTS

The concept of neurodiversity challenges our perception of what normal, typical, or average is. Not all children and adults learn to read when exposed to one type of teaching. An example of this is phonic-based reading programmes, which have been hailed as the way to teach all children to read. While such programmes remain a robust approach to teaching reading skills for many, they are now recognised as not the only route to reading.

Each student will vary in their rates of development and acquisition of skills, and consequently we will need to vary our approaches to teaching and learning. In one class you may have one student who is slower at developing reading skills and may still be struggling at a word level, and there may be a higher-performing student who is a fluent reader with advanced comprehension skills. However, it is also possible that you may encounter a child who struggles to decode text and finds reading tiring, but also has heightened skills in terms of their ability to analyse and identify meaning. They could be seen as slower reader, but quicker thinker.

In order to optimise someone's skills, you need to identify and choose varied techniques and experiment with different tools to find the best fit. We need to consider variation in patterns of challenges and strengths as these do not often cluster neatly. All children with dyslexia will be different and assumptions cannot be made. Some students may have challenges with spelling alone and others with reading and writing, for example. When adjustments are made this can also open opportunities for better engagement and change the way we view that student's potential. A student who is allowed to dictate or use speech-to-text software may suddenly be able to produce rich content and use more elaborate words and phrasing.

There is evidence that some students with Down's syndrome have very specific patterns of reading skills and may typically have an uneven profile with stronger visual than verbal skills, stronger receptive vocabulary than expressive language and grammatical skills, and strengths in reading abilities. Another student may be verbally able but has challenges putting their ideas on to paper. What we may see in common in each of these students is that they get bored and disaffected by a one-size-fits-all approach.

Some other examples of neurodivergent students not fitting education include:

- the fidgety student who finds it hard to sit still for long in an English class may do better in classes such as science where they can stand and move around more and participate actively;
- the student who has difficulties with handwriting may be disruptive because they are embarrassed for others to see their writing when they need to record information and, as a result, produce little written work but may be verbally able and vocalise great ideas in class discussion;
- the student who requires longer to process information, reflect and respond may not perform so well in a timed exam but does much better when given a written assignment;
- the student who needs information repeated or broken down and loses meaning if the pace is too fast, or who may appear to be frustrated or disinterested, but does well if information is also provided visually by their teacher.

We will discuss throughout the book – above all in **Chapters 7 and 8** – how we need to vary our approaches to teaching, learning and assessment so that we don't favour some learners' skills more than others. This is particularly important when we consider that the skills society values are socially constructed and are likely to change over time.

THE NEURODIVERGENT STUDENT AND CHANGING ENVIRONMENTS

As students move through the educational system the environment becomes more complex and the demands on each student will increase. The external factors in our lives, such as where we are studying or working, and the demands of others, can either positively or negatively influence our outcomes.

There is extensive research showing that students with ADHD, dyslexia and developmental coordination disorder experience increased levels of executive functioning challenges. This can result in them having greater challenges with planning, self-organisation and regulating their emotions. These are the exact skills you need as you progress through education and eventually into employment. While some neurodivergent individuals may find tasks requiring good executive functioning more challenging, we know that, with the right support and strategies put in place, such barriers can either be removed or reduced. It is important to recognise that different ways of thinking may also result in a student generating an alternative way to solve a problem that may not even have previously been considered by the teacher!

A move from primary school to secondary school will require greater self-organisational skills. In high school the student may begin to travel independently to a bigger school, move from class to class and have an array of teachers with different teaching styles and approaches. These changes also require that the student has the right kit with them, can plan their work and meet deadlines.

As educators we may see a student who has coped reasonably well in primary school quickly start to struggle when they transition from primary to secondary school. We need to ensure that transition planning starts early enough and recognise that increasing demands, and a changing environment, may be tipping points for some students. By doing this in a timely manner, the parent, teacher and individual can help each student meet their potential.

In adulthood, in addition to studying or working, we usually need to manage our home, social and work lives. This requires good planning and time management skills and the ability to juggle priorities. Taking a lifelong approach to supporting neurodivergent students is essential. We explore further in later chapters how strategies which work can often be adapted to be used in different contexts so that students have access to transferable strategies they can call on throughout their lives.

We also need to consider the adults who are in and interact with our educational ecosystems and who are neurodivergent as well. For example, we know that around 20 per cent of parents of children with ADHD will also have ADHD. In **Chapter 10** we will discuss more about how to support neurodivergent teachers – and teachers working with parents – in education workplaces, and consider what adjustments may be helpful.

The concept of neurodiversity coined by Singer and Blume provides a rationale for considering how we must support all students and create settings that are more inclusive. Embracing this language positively and consistently across education, health and other services means we can develop a framework for action. We will discuss these frameworks throughout this book. Understanding the concept of neurodiversity and recognising the importance of inclusivity is important, otherwise we could end up with neurodiversity being associated once again with deficit and disorder rather than harnessing our differences.

KEY TAKEAWAYS

- Neurodiversity is about us all and is not associated with one specific condition.
- Neurodiversity describes the different ways that we all think, move, process information, hear, see, understand and communicate with each other. We are all neurodiverse.
- You can be born with neurodivergent traits or acquire them throughout life.
- We can have both strengths and challenges which will vary from person to person.
- Our environment can change over time and may result in increased demands on executive functioning skills which may make it more challenging at times of transition for those who are neurodivergent.
- The environment in which we live, study and work influences what we see as typical (or not) and this can shape our ability to engage or disengage in education.

2

FRAMING NEURODIVERSITY: PAST AND PRESENT

In this chapter we will consider:

- the history of neurodiversity in the context of education moving from predominantly using a medical model of practice, with narrow definitions for specific conditions, to the use of a much broader understanding and recognition that overlap between conditions is common;
- some of the practical challenges for educators in enacting inclusive processes, and examples of how some have tried to embrace this;
- the importance of common terminology, and that neurodiversity framing may be an opportunity for educators to take person-centred approaches to ensure there is support for all and remove the need for the term 'special' from the educational vocabulary.

SOCIETY'S VIEWS OF 'SPECIAL' STUDENTS

Different terms have been used to group students who learn differently from the 'average student', depending on the knowledge, understanding, political, medical, social, cultural, or educational trends and practices of the time. It is important, therefore, to recognise that our understanding of neurodivergence has been shaped and somewhat skewed by the trends, values and norms of each respective period. For a long time, we have recognised there are some students who have found it problematic to engage fully in a one-size-fits-all educational system. Throughout history, people who did not conform to or fit in with societal norms have often been treated differently. We have used terms such as 'specific', 'remedial', 'different', 'disorder', 'deficit' and 'disabled'.

The language we use to describe students who learn differently from the social norm of the time is important not only in how people view themselves but also in how others view them. Our views and the terms we have used have not always been the most positive, or indeed accurate. For example, in Roman and mediaeval times, people with physical disabilities, mental illness or intellectual deficiency were labelled as 'fools' and court jesters and employed to entertain nobility. In more recent times in Nazi Germany, children who were severely mentally and 'physically handicapped' were classified as 'lives unworthy of life' (*Lebensunwertes Leben*) and would be 'eliminated'. This demonstrates the potentially dangerous ramifications where specific societies have a more limited or skewed understanding of difference.

Some cultures and countries in the past have taken a more positive view of people with disabilities. For example, among Dahomeans of West Africa, infants born with disabilities were often believed to be the result of supernatural forces, said to be good luck, and were seen to safeguard others from evil spirits and misfortune.

20TH- AND 21ST-CENTURY PERSPECTIVES OF INCLUSION

Our views of difference in society have changed considerably. The language related to neurodiversity recognises the differences in us all and is pertinent for education today. We have seen several global initiatives promoting an inclusive approach to education and aiming to support all students equitably. The UNESCO Convention in 1960 focused on discrimination in education and was followed by other international human rights treaties. The aim of such policies was to prohibit any exclusion from, or limitation to, educational opportunities based on socially ascribed or perceived differences. The UNESCO Convention aimed to promote inclusive education systems that remove the barriers limiting the participation and achievement of all learners. Although these are internationally recognised treaties, there have been varying interpretations from one country to another of what defines learners' needs and how to deliver inclusive education.

The phrase 'special educational needs' (or SEN) is first thought to have been used in the UK in the Warnock Report in the late 1970s. Dame Mary Warnock was tasked to examine the educational needs of all children and young people who were seen as 'handicapped by disabilities of body and mind' and to establish a general conceptual framework within which provision could be made. She made an important point in the *British Medical Journal* at the time, that if the local education authorities were 'to have the duty to educate *all* children in *ordinary* schools' there was a need for increased and different training for teachers (Warnock, 1979, p. 667, emphasis added). She also highlighted that education could create barriers to access.

Warnock importantly described the importance of considering the ecology of the student not only in school but in their home settings. She sowed the seeds for us to think about the individual in the context of their environment, which we discuss throughout this book.

TEACHING INCLUDES EVERYONE

Both the Warnock Report and the 1981 UK Education Act made important contributions that altered the conceptualisation of 'special education' by emphasising that a child's educational *need* should be prioritised, rather than their individual learning disability or impairment. Educational institutions were told that teachers had a role to teach *all* students, and that schools had a role to reduce obstacles for learning. This also meant teachers were now required to consider more person-centred approaches to teaching rather than one approach for all.

In 1994 the World Conference on Special Needs Education was held in Salamanca in Spain. The resulting framework called for inclusion to be the norm, stating that 'inclusion and participation are essential to human dignity and to the enjoyment and exercise of human rights' (Ministerio de Educación y Ciencia de España, 1994, p. 11). Education policies and practices changed in many countries, even though in reality the concepts were often poorly understood and only partially implemented.

Special needs education aimed to incorporate proven methods of teaching from which all children could benefit. However, adaptations were largely seen as something that happened outside the classroom. While guidance such as the Warnock Report promoted greater access for pupils with SEN to mainstream education, many students still did not experience full participation while learning within the classroom setting.

In the 21st century we have laid the foundations for change in the form of global policy and legislation, for example in the paper *Education for all* from UNESCO and the Convention on the Rights of Persons with Disabilities, which was the first comprehensive human rights treaty adopted by the United Nations in 2006. Two of the UN's latest documents, including *Sustainable Development Goal 4* on education and the *Education 2030 Framework for Action*, emphasise inclusion and equity as laying the foundations for quality education.

Yet to make real progress and ensure we meet these objectives in a way that is impactful, we need to support teachers and educators to develop their practice considering universal design principles as a means of delivery. There is often a disconnect between policy and how teachers are meant to translate this into meaningful practice in the classroom. We will provide some practical tools to do so in later chapters and discuss this in more detail in **Chapter 5**.

WHAT MODELS DO WE USE TO IDENTIFY SUPPORT NEEDS?

The field of neurodisability research has contributed several theoretical frameworks to try to understand an individual and the challenges they may have in accessing and participating in education, and more broadly in society.

The different models have changed and evolved over time and represent the knowledge and values of that point in history. Understanding the development of such models helps us to understand better how educational practices, and indeed society's views, have progressed.

It is important to consider all models in the field of neurodiversity particularly in terms of how they have shaped perceived values and norms. The medical model remains dominant in the educational context, whereby a student often only gains support once a diagnosis has been obtained. But taking this approach can leave groups of students being misunderstood, misdiagnosed, or missing out altogether in gaining support (3Ms). We will describe why this happens in more detail in the next chapter.

THE MEDICAL MODEL

The medical model sees challenges or impairment residing within the individual or student. A child who can't engage in lessons needs help to focus; a student who has difficulties with recording information may have DCD. The doctor, or other health care professionals, are usually central to making a diagnosis as they generally are the ones compiling the information and assessments and diagnosing specific conditions such as ASC. The professionals look for specific symptoms and signs that fit with an agreed set of criteria for each condition. Part of making a diagnosis will also be to rule out other conditions. The basis of the diagnosis of ADHD, ASC, DLD, DCD and tic disorders, for example, is very much based on a deficit-based approach.

As we mentioned in **Chapter 1**, researchers have also followed this approach and spent many years trying to find genes relating to single conditions, which has only reinforced the medical model as a predominant way of viewing difference.

Paediatricians, psychologists and neurologists in the first part of the 20th century (and even earlier) described children and young people who were considered to diverge from the social norm of the time. Some children would stay for long periods of time in a sanatorium or hospital, and this allowed the doctors extensive time to observe and describe specific behaviours of the children in their care.

Professional success and kudos were often rated on the ability to be the first to publish their thinking. The prolonged and close observation allowed for early classification of specific behaviours and resulted in physicians having 'disorders' named after them. While the medical field was dominated by men, interestingly, some females who were also at the forefront of scientific discoveries were often forgotten. Grunya Sukhareva was one of these people and was a Russian Jewish doctor who published her findings about autism nearly two decades before Hans Asperger did, but it is the latter whose name is still associated with the condition. This narrow framing and naming are rarely done today in this way. Diagnostic criteria are internationally agreed and re-evaluated regularly, with specialists pooling their experiences and basing their decisions on the current, shared clinical and research findings.

From the mid-20th century onwards, clinicians started recognising that many children they met didn't fit into specific diagnostic boxes and had a variety of symptoms and signs that crossed over the narrower categorisations. Helmer Myklebust, a prominent US psychologist, in 1964 described specific learning disabilities as 'the result of minor disturbances of brain function' (Boshes & Myklebust, 1964, p. 7) and he suggested the use of the term 'psychoneurological' to indicate that he thought that disabilities were the psychological representation of a number of neurological deficits.

Around a similar time, other terms were also being used to try to group and organise different and varying cognitive presentations. Terms such as *minimal brain dysfunction* (MBD), *minor neurological dysfunction* (MND) and *minimal cerebral dysfunction* were coined. The MBD framing, for example, recognised a group of children with 'normal' intelligence but who had varying combinations of perception, language, attention, impulse control and motor control challenges. This term was criticised by paediatricians, including the eminent child psychiatrist, Michael Rutter.

Other terms followed, such as *disorders of attention, motor and perception* (or DAMP), which was coined in the 1980s by Swedish paediatrician Christopher Gillberg. Many of these terms have not been widely adopted or liked by parents, who understandably don't want a diagnosis describing their child as DAMP or, to use another example, having a 'minimal brain'! The terms themselves are not very helpful as they are vague and in many ways take us further away from forming an accurate understanding.

The US Individuals with Disabilities Education Act (revised, 2019) now defines specific learning disabilities as:

> a disorder in one or more of the basic cognitive processes involved in understanding or in using language, spoken or written, which disorder may manifest itself in the imperfect ability to listen, think, speak, read, write, spell, or do mathematical calculations.
>
> (US Government, *IDEA*, Section 1401 (30))

THE SOCIAL MODEL

In contrast to the medical model, the social model, described first by Mike Oliver in the 1990s, states that we are not disabled by our impairments but *by the disabling barriers presented by society*. The social model therefore recognised the interrelationship between an individual and their environment and sought to emphasise the need to take action in the removal of barriers that may undermine an individual's ability to access, participate and make progress in society. An obvious example of this could be changing the physical environment to allow access for a person to a building by providing a ramp as well as steps.

THE BIOPSYCHOSOCIAL MODEL

A third model is the biopsychosocial model, which was first described in the late 1970s and is conceptually an extension of the social model. It considers three intersecting factors – the biological, psychological and social aspects to the individual:

- bio (physiological pathology such as genes, physical and psychological health);

- psycho (thoughts, emotions and behaviours such as psychological distress, fear/avoidance beliefs, current coping methods and attribution);
- social (socio-economical, socio-environmental and cultural factors such as school issues, family circumstances and social setting).

The biopsychosocial model emphasises the need for an interdisciplinary way of working across different professionals and stresses the interconnectedness of the different factors (see Figure 2.1).

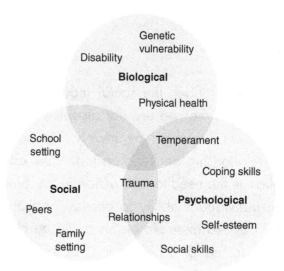

Figure 2.1   Biopsychosocial model

THE ECOLOGICAL SYSTEMS MODEL

The ecological systems model considers the role that the wider ecology of the student plays in shaping their past and present and how this enables the student to access and be included in education – or the opposite. It also considers changes that may happen across time (see Figure 2.2). This model was first described by psychologist Urie Bronfenbrenner, and we will consider it in further detail in **Chapter 3**.

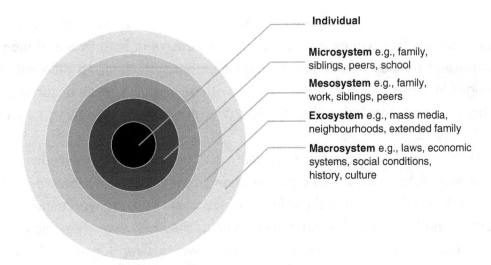

Figure 2.2   Ecological systems model (Bronfenbrenner)

It is interesting to reflect on the different models over time and how they have shaped the traits and conditions we now associate with neurodiversity. By doing so, we have a greater insight into the rationale for exploring the principles of universal design.

SILOED APPROACHES

Despite some clinicians recognising a cluster of symptoms and signs co-occurring together, the single-condition focus by research and clinical practices dominated till the late 1990s. Even today, despite knowing that overlap or co-occurrence between conditions commonly exists, many health and educational professionals continue to work in silos with their specific areas of knowledge and expertise.

The approach by different professionals to support different 'parts' of a student has resulted in parents often having to go from one specialist to another, frustratingly repeating information in different places and at different times. It often means only one diagnosis is considered at a time and is a reason why some challenges get missed all together, as we shall see in the next chapter. This can be exhausting and expensive in both time and money for parents as they must wade through different systems using different language. In terms of educational support, it can mean a focus according to *label* and not considering the student's overall needs or the setting they live and study in.

We also now recognise that the pattern and presentation of neurodivergent traits may not remain stable and can change over time. For example, someone with ADHD will often show fewer of the overt signs of hyperactivity and have a greater sense of 'inner restlessness' as they get older. They may have busy thoughts and find it harder to settle down to sleep for example. Their symptoms may also change as the demands of executive functioning increase and they need to manage themselves and their work. Another example of change could be a child who first gets diagnosed with speech and language delay at a younger age and then dyslexia as they get older when the demands of understanding and recording information increase.

In more recent times, Christopher Gillberg (2010) and colleagues coined the acronym ESSENCE, standing for *early symptomatic syndromes eliciting neurodevelopmental clinical examinations*. It has been used to group children with overlapping but variable neurodevelopmental challenges. ESSENCE refers to the whole group of neurodevelopmental or neuropsychiatric disorders that present with impairing symptoms in early childhood, and includes ADHD, ASC, developmental coordination disorder, developmental language disorder, Tourette's syndrome, early onset bipolar disorder and a variety of neurological and seizure disorders presenting with major behavioural or cognitive problems at an early age. ESSENCE once again tries to represent a positioning that many of these conditions rarely present alone.

Today, health and educational professionals and researchers are finally agreeing that there is a need to move from a categorical viewpoint where we look at each condition as if it operates in isolation to recognising that the edges are blurred between conditions such as autism and ADHD, and are taking a more multidimensional approach. In some countries we are starting to see health service approaches providers delivering neurodevelopmental pathways with greater interdisciplinary working. This means health professionals not only working with other health professionals from different backgrounds but also working in a transdisciplinary manner with educational and social practitioners. This provides the opportunity to bring information from multiple sources together to deliver truly person-centred care. It also allows for planning in education and provides feedback to health professionals on the impact of interventions that have been put in place.

MOVING TO SPECTRA AND DIMENSIONS

Not only have we changed our understanding of developmental conditions, but we are starting to consider how we need to understand the ecology of the student now and previously. We are beginning to recognise the spectra of neurodivergent traits that represent the varying differences and strengths we see from one student to another. We are taking a more multidimensional approach. Today, rather than a dominant focus on causation, we are considering far more the impact on learning from genes, alongside interactions with our environment.

WHAT DOES THIS ALL MEAN FOR EDUCATION?

Despite global initiatives and recognition of overlap between neurodivergent conditions, and while progress is being made in some places in developing diagnostic pathways, there is still some way to go before inclusion is common practice. In many countries we still see the medical model as the dominant pathway to gaining recognition of need and consequent support. We will see in **Chapter 3** who misses out if we take this approach.

Access to diagnosis remains inequitable, and hard to understand and navigate. In many cases it is determined by the ability to pay for services. This leaves many parents waiting years to have their child seen by a health professional, if at all. The delay in gaining support to be able to participate fully in education (and more broadly in society) may lead to students experiencing increasing frustration and educational failure. It can also lead to secondary consequences arising for both the student and the family, including an impact on mental wellbeing.

We are still witnessing the segregation of students with 'special' educational needs in a range of ways. Too often students are described as having social, emotional and academic needs, especially in the US, Australia and the UK, and end up being excluded from school. This is happening in growing numbers. Different terms are used to describe support, including 'alternative provision' where children have been removed from a 'mainstream setting' into what have ironically been called 'inclusion' units. We also move some students even further away from mainstream settings. Some children such as those with autism and intellectual disabilities continue to be placed in 'special' schools and 'specialist' units. There is more work to be done through education, training and taking time to understand students' real needs more comprehensively.

KEY TAKEAWAYS

- There has been changing use and understanding of different terms over time: neurodiversity is a framing for the modern day.
- There is increasing recognition that the named conditions and the silos we used in the past are no longer fit for purpose and can inaccurately pigeonhole a student and miss out vital information about their strengths as well as the overall picture of their challenges.
- The categorical approach is not a reality and co-occurrence among conditions and behaviours is the norm.
- In the context of educational provision, the term 'special educational need' has a legal definition that refers to children who have learning difficulties and/or disabilities, which make it more difficult for them to learn or access education than most children of the same age.

- We need to consider whether the term 'special needs' is about disability rights as when the law of the land recognises someone as deserving rights, it gives a term power.
- Students, like everyone else, have complex and multidimensional presentations resulting from their interaction with genes and environment, meaning that each student has a unique pattern of strengths and challenges that can change over time.

3

THE 3Ms: MISSED, MISDIAGNOSED AND MISUNDERSTOOD

In this chapter we will consider:

- how the environment in which a child develops can impact on their learning;
- which students get missed, misunderstood or misdiagnosed, and so miss out on gaining the support they need;
- the reasons for this, including race, gender and disadvantage;
- the societal barriers and interferences that impact on the individual and their family.

Most of us would prefer clearly defined pathways for support: if we see a challenge with X, then Y happens next. However, the reality is that the route to support can be winding and not always clearly signposted. Concerns regarding a student's progress may come from parents, health professionals, social services, educators and the student themselves. When, where and which barriers get identified can lead to the student taking a different pathway, resulting in very different outcomes educationally and in life.

A STUDENT'S ECOLOGY

To understand a student's ecology, it is useful to use a framework. We featured some models in the last chapter, including the one by the American psychologist, Urie Bronfenbrenner, who proposed the 'ecological systems theory'. His theory is a useful one in the context of neurodiversity. He viewed child development as a complex system of relationships affected by multiple levels of the surrounding environment, from immediate settings of family and school to broad cultural values, laws and customs.

Not only does a student's ecological context affect their level of functioning, but it will also directly shape the support they are able to access and impact significantly on their ability to overcome barriers and fulfil their potential. Many students run the risk of their support needs being missed altogether or, if identified, being misdiagnosed and their needs being misunderstood (see Figure 3.1).

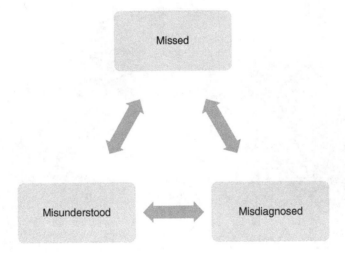

Figure 3.1   The 3 Ms

Bronfenbrenner divided the person's environment into five different systems: the microsystem, the mesosystem, the exosystem, the macrosystem and the chronosystem. The microsystem is the most influential level of the ecological systems theory. It contains the most immediate environmental settings for the developing child, such as their family and school. By understanding the interaction between the various systems, we can not only see how they link together but also how some students can fall through the gaps of service provision.

Figure 3.2 is an adapted version of Bronfenbrenner's ecological systems model, showing the series of interacting systems that impact on the outcomes for a child or young person. The interactions are not linear or equal in engagement or impact. For example, changes to the law by the government can impact directly on a neurodivergent student tomorrow in terms of the support they receive, but other changes may evolve over a longer period of time. Although services such as police, youth work and housing sit at a similar level in this diagram, they do not all communicate with each other or deliver combined, personalised support for one person with multiple needs. This can have more impact on the pathway one student takes compared to another.

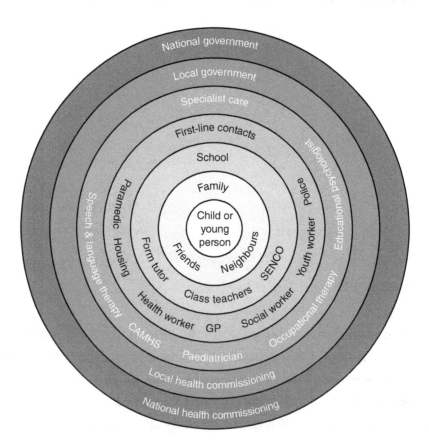

Figure 3.2   Adapted version of Bronfenbrenner's ecological systems model

PATHWAYS TO SUPPORT VARY

A very frequent experience for many neurodivergent students is that they only get noticed in school if their behaviours disrupt others. An example of this could be a student answering out of turn or being fidgety and annoying others by their movements or getting into an argument with another student. This can often lead to educators becoming focused on solving the behaviour-related challenges, rather than stepping back and considering the underlying reasons for the behaviours.

By pausing and considering the 4 Ws (see Figure 3.3) we can consider some of the many reasons for some of the behaviours we may notice.

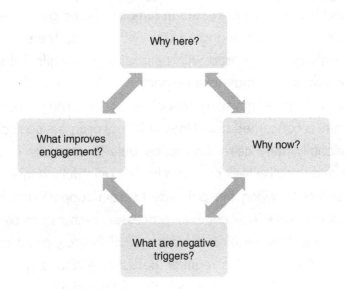

Figure 3.3   The 4 Ws

- *Why here?* Is this a particular lesson the student has challenges with? Is this with one teacher?
- *Why now?* Is the lesson at the end of the day, so the student may be more tired and less able to focus? Is the student sitting with a particular student? Has the teaching content changed or got harder? Is their externalising behaviour worse after a weekend or when they come in from lunch breaks?

- *What are negative triggers?* Has the student been asked to copy down some work and finds writing difficult? Has the task changed, and the student hasn't had time to change their thinking and pace to a new task? Has the student just eaten?
- *What improves engagement?* Is it when the student is doing something they have a specific interest in, or is allowed to talk about their ideas? Is it better when they work with other students or with a specific student? Does the student engage in some lessons more than others?

Some students may not be noticed at all. In contrast to the student externalising their thoughts and feelings, some students may withdraw from social interactions, especially when anxious, or mask how they really feel by trying to fit in. It is harder to recognise how someone is feeling when they have more internalising behaviours, and this is more prevalent in females. Some girls may demonstrate anxiety by being quiet and engaging less with others. There is evidence that females often only get diagnosed with neurodivergent traits if their challenges are much worse than their male counterparts or if there are other challenges or manifestations, such as self-harming, school refusal or having an eating disorder.

Even if a parent is concerned about their child not progressing socially, emotionally or educationally, they need then to be able to navigate educational and health systems and vocalise their concerns in a meaningful manner. The challenge for some parents is knowing the pathway to gain support and being able to engage in what are sometimes complex processes, such as completing challenging paperwork. This often requires a high level of literacy, good communication and organisational skills. It also requires persistence and engagement in often lengthy assessments. This may have additional financial implications for some parents if they must take time off work to attend appointments.

NOT EVERYONE STARTS FROM THE SAME POINT

Not everyone starts from the same point educationally and some children are at a greater disadvantage. Poverty, and the impact this has on educational attainment, was highlighted globally during the Covid-19 pandemic. Lower socio-economic status often results in less parental resource, including lack of access to technology, which can be of real assistance to students today. This can again be a reason for students being missed.

Despite an increasing awareness of neurodivergent traits, there are many parents who are also neurodivergent but who have so far not been diagnosed or gained any support. This may mean they have similar challenges with literacy, organisation or communication skills as their children, and this can impact on how they support their children. If we can support parents with gaining the appropriate skills, the outcomes for their child can improve.

Neurodivergent parents (without a diagnosis) may have assumed their child is 'just like them', and consider this as the family norm, and not be aware of support that is now available. Their own challenges may impact on their child as well. A family member with ADHD traits may struggle with self-organisation, resulting in them finding it harder to organise their child's work, help with homework or be on time for appointments. A parent with reading challenges may read less to their child. This can have a secondary impact on readiness for school, such as arriving with some pre-literacy skills in place.

In the 1990s, researchers Betty Hart and Todd Risley studied families from different socio-economic levels in the US and found that children were exposed to vastly different numbers of words in their early years. Amazingly, 32 million more words were spoken to their children by parents from higher-income households than those coming from lower-income households. The variability in exposure accounted for significant differences in children's language skills when they entered kindergarten, and this had a direct impact on how students progressed early on in their school life. We don't know how many parents who did not read to their children were dyslexic themselves.

A 2018 study led by researchers at Harvard and Massachusetts Institute of Technology (MIT) used fMRI technology to track how children's brains reacted while they listened to stories. They found that young children who had more frequent conversations with their caregivers had different neurological patterns than peers who didn't. Only by recognising and working with the whole family early on in a child's life can we make changes for future generations of learners.

HEALTH OUTCOMES VARY GLOBALLY AND CAN IMPACT EDUCATIONALLY

Rates of neurodivergent conditions vary across the globe. There are several reasons for this including socio-economic inequality. Globally, more than 80 per cent of the world's births occur in low- and middle-income countries (LAMIC), but importantly most of the epidemiological research relating to neurodiversity is based on data from Western, educated, industrialised, rich and democratic countries (WEIRD). There are few studies on the epidemiology of neurodevelopmental conditions and related disability in LAMIC, where the burden could be greatest because the incidence of risk factors for disability such as perinatal complications, head injury, parasitic infections and nutritional deficiencies are higher, according to the reported global burden of disease studies. Research, dominated by the West, has used a narrow lens through which to draw its conclusions. When developing educational solutions, we need to consider what the true picture is and what the implications for learning are in LAMIC countries.

In the UK, a recent analysis of 1 million births estimated that 24 per cent of stillbirths, 19 per cent of pre-term births and 31 per cent of foetal growth retardation cases were attributed to socio-economic inequality, and would not have occurred if all women had the same risk of adverse pregnancy outcomes as women in the least-deprived group. These factors have implications for rates of presentation and the identification of neurodivergent traits.

Another reason for increasing rates of neurodivergent traits today compared to the past may be because of successful treatment interventions and advances in healthcare, including vaccination programmes. Over the past ten to 15 years children have survived who would not have done so in the past. There is evidence of higher risk of learning challenges being present in very premature babies. Higher numbers of neurodivergent children being present in the classroom today than would have been seen in the past may be a secondary consequence of them surviving because of these medical advancements. These represent in some ways a new group of neurodivergent students.

AWARENESS AND ACCESS TO SERVICES VARIES GLOBALLY

Awareness and access to services may make a difference in terms of identification. A worldwide review showed that the prevalence rate of ADHD worldwide is just over 5 per cent but there are wide variations from 7–10 per cent in Asia, 4–10 per cent in Africa and 4–6 per cent in Latin America. Rates in Europe are significantly lower than rates in North America.

This may be for several reasons. There is higher awareness of ADHD in the US, which may lead to earlier identification and more services. UK guidelines on identification are more prescriptive which means that fewer children will reach the threshold for diagnosis. There are also gaps in service provision across the UK, resulting in fewer children gaining a diagnosis. Identification may put some US children at an educational advantage as support may be successfully put in place. This inconsistency in provision and access to services highlights a very real challenge globally; in some countries, there are few or no services for some conditions at all.

DIFFERENT EXPERIENCES END UP IN DIFFERENT SUPPORT

There are many different factors that we need to consider when understanding why a student may not be progressing at the same pace as other students in the class.

VARIATION IN DEVELOPMENT

Most of us recognise deviation and variation in motor and language development. We know that two children born on the same day in the same hospital can end up walking at very different times. One child can be doing so at nine months and the other six months later. On the one hand, both may be neurotypical. On the other hand, one of the first signs of neurodivergent traits may be significant delay in movement or language. A child may also have inconsistent patterns of development and can be neurotypical in one area of development such as movement but have a delay with language development. This is an illustration of the 'spiky profile' we mentioned in **Chapter 1**. Additionally, we need to remind ourselves that development is not linear. We can also see that different students may approach learning very differently but reach the same outcomes in different ways.

VARIATION IN PARENTING PRACTICES

Parenting practices vary globally and can result in differences in child development rates and pathways that don't appear to be detrimental to long-term development. For example, toilet training may vary from country to country. Parents in China often begin their children's toilet training soon after birth and dress them in something like open-crotch pants, while in the UK toilet training may not start before the age of two.

Comparison of development is often made depending on the cultural expectations and norms of that country. It's important we do not ignore cultural variations when considering if a child is demonstrating neurodivergent traits and only consider developmental norms from a Western perspective. We could be making false assumptions about the development of a child which may in fact be typical for that culture and setting. This is another example of potential misdiagnosis.

VARIATIONS IN OPPORTUNITIES FOR ATTACHMENT

There are some emotional life experiences that can have a long-term detrimental impact on development, wherever they take place in the world. More than 30 years ago, Romanian orphanages were exposed as places where some children were placed in the 'hospital for irrecoverables'. Children who had been born without apparent challenges were neglected and lacked stimulation, and so ended up with enduring emotional and physical disability. A recent study of twins from Sweden identified more than 8,000 nine-year-olds, and showed that the children who had been subjected to maltreatment had a greater number of neurodevelopmental challenges than those who had not been maltreated. There is no doubt that exposure and opportunities for learning and exploring are important for all children's development.

There has been some debate whether the focus on early intervention programmes dismisses or hides the underlying issue of social inequity which also exists. It is important that when we recognise some neurodivergence from the typical social norms we explore the reasons why. What we know, for example, is that two children starting school who have a difference in age of as much as 11 months are usually at different stages of development. The very youngest child can experience greater academic disadvantage. Interestingly, because of this understanding the UK brought out guidance in 2020 on differentiating starting times across the school year.

Let's consider in more detail three specific groups where the direction of educational travel can vary and neurodivergent traits may be missed, misunderstood or misdiagnosed altogether, and the many reasons for this.

MISSED

Our system of diagnoses of specific conditions has been predicated on being 'bad enough' to gain a diagnosis. People must have sufficient symptoms and signs to meet a threshold for a diagnosis. The threshold may vary from country to country and within a country. Gaining support and intervention has been based on a principle of all or nothing.

This means that those who fall just below the line don't get support. The concept of the 'balls in the bucket' explains this (see Figure 3.4). Systems also favour some types of 'cognitive balls' over others. If your challenges are in an area where there is greater awareness and access to support, you will gain more help. If this is not the case, then you may not gain any support at all.

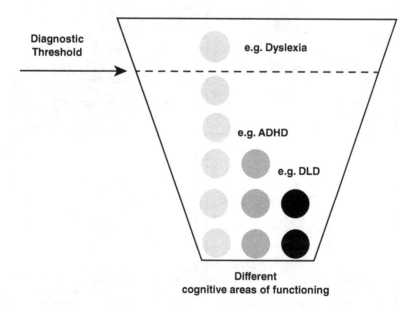

Figure 3.4   Balls in the bucket (Kirby, 2022)

THE PROFESSIONAL LENSES WE LOOK THROUGH DIFFER

Our training may lead us to making different assumptions about whether a student has challenges that fit into one particular box. Figure 3.5 represents the different lenses we may look through when considering an individual student, depending on our understanding and knowledge. The parent may see certain behaviours only at home and there may also be housing challenges which mean the student is finding it difficult to study in the evenings. School may see a student struggling to learn to read, write or focus on their lessons. Someone else, such as a psychologist, may be presented with a student who is angry and anxious. However, if we extend this metaphor a little and see this as a kaleidoscope and then turn the dial to align all the views, we can see the whole student.

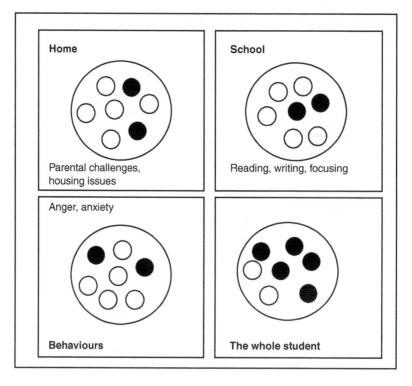

Figure 3.5   Professional lenses

Until recently, the diagnosis of neurodevelopmental conditions has been far greater in males than females. For example, males are diagnosed with autism spectrum condition (ASC) approximately four times as often as females. Psychiatrists and family doctors globally have less knowledge about how females present with symptoms and signs of ADHD and ASC.

They have also had less training in neurodevelopmental conditions and often have not had a deep understanding of how neurodivergent traits co-occur with mental health conditions. Consequently, females may have gained a diagnosis of one or more mental health conditions, such as anxiety, substance misuse, self-harm or eating disorders. This doesn't mean they don't have the mental health challenges, but ADHD and ASC may not have been considered in the mix. It may also be one of the reasons why many females are only being identified as neurodivergent in adulthood. We explore the association with mental health in more detail in **Chapter 4**.

The bias in diagnosis is called *ascertainment bias* and refers to males being more likely to be referred for assessment than females with equivalent challenges. As we highlighted earlier in the chapter, on the one hand, more boys may end up being referred with reading problems because they openly express frustration and exhibit more hyperactive and disruptive behaviours in the classroom. Females may, on the other hand, be missed because of the 'type' of ADHD traits they have: the predominantly inattentive ADHD 'dreamy' type usually creates less disruption for others. Girls may be seen doodling, taking longer to complete tasks, quietly whispering to their peers, or even showing prosocial behaviour by offering to help in class because they easily get bored. By offering to help it allows them to move around and stops them feeling so fidgety. However, it is only recently that we have recognised that these are different behaviours in females that can alert us to ADHD and autism.

Teacher knowledge is important for correct identification. In one study of primary school teachers in 2014 researchers found that teachers frequently did not identify the inattentive ADHD type and were not aware that medication could be helpful in this context (Moldavsky et al., 2014). Another study from Sweden identified bias in reporting of ADHD characteristics by gender of the adult observing the children. Male adult participants in the study reported ADHD characteristics more in boys and more accurately, and female adults reported girls with ADHD more accurately. As a result of these varying factors, females may have less opportunity to gain a diagnosis.

Females who are on the autism spectrum also tend to be diagnosed at an older age than males. This may be because we have usually seen autism through a male lens and were looking for male-like symptoms rather than considering how autism presents in females. Females are more often better at 'camouflaging' or masking, and emulate the social behaviours of other girls around them. However, this can result in the child becoming exhausted or having an emotional meltdown when they get home from school because they have been 'compensating' all day. It's a bit like holding your breath, you can only do it for so long before you must stop and let it all out!

Gender bias in diagnosis has been noted in other conditions including developmental co-ordination disorder (also known as dyspraxia). One survey of elementary school teachers showed that they were more likely to report concerns about the gross motor skills performance of boys than the fine motor performance of girls, and considered it more important to intervene with the children with gross motor problems. Sporting skills were seen in the past as more important for boys, so a lack of skills may have been noted more often in boys while some girls were having similar challenges. This may have meant that girls were less likely to be considered as having DCD at all. We will explore in later chapters how we can reframe our assumptions about what common behaviours associated with a specific label might look like so that we can view everyone more holistically.

MISDIAGNOSED

A lack of recognition and support may result in negative consequences for those whose needs are unmet. Research describes that where there has been a lack of identification of ADHD, autism, DLD or DCD, the result has been secondary consequences for the individuals in both the short and longer term. For example, not engaging with peers or being misunderstood can lead to lowered self-esteem and increased anxiety. As a consequence, a student may be less able to focus academically and have a greater chance of educational failure or reduced employment opportunities.

Some cognitive behaviours are also valued and attract more support than others. A diagnosis of autism may be seen as a 'golden ticket' as it often results in parents obtaining dedicated support for their child. The level of support may be related to the specific label and not have anything to do with level of actual need. Work by researchers in the UK in 2019 showed that children with a label of autism with lower levels of language challenges got more speech and language support than those with a more severe developmental language disorder but who did *not* have the diagnosis of autism.

Another example of misdiagnosis is one that happens when we only consider attention-deficit hyperactivity disorder. Students may present with difficulties with attention and concentration which may be related to traumatic brain injury (TBI) from years before. Longitudinal research has shown that children who have a TBI before the age of three are significantly more likely to have ADHD, autism spectrum condition, or developmental delay in later childhood (Chang et al., 2018). Amir Sariaslan and colleagues published another study in 2016 where they followed up more than a million people who had sustained a head injury before the age of 25 years and they showed that there was lasting impact on educational outcomes, sleep, planning, organisation and social behaviour. There are high rates of TBI in offending populations and the relationship between this and learning has often not been considered.

MISUNDERSTOOD

Initial teacher training will vary in the focus on typical child development, and may focus more on information relating to dyslexia and dyscalculia and less on some conditions such as DCD and DLD, despite them commonly co-occurring. This may be because education has traditionally been weighted more towards literacy and maths.

A teacher who has had more training related to social, emotional and mental health than neurodiversity may consider attachment and behavioural issues in a child before thinking about alternative reasons (see again Figure 3.4). For example, there are high rates of undiagnosed communication challenges and ADHD in children excluded from school. Misunderstood behaviours may result in a 'school to prison pipeline'. Sadly, at least one in three people in prison are neurodivergent but most have never had their needs identified. Many have also experienced other adverse events that have impacted on their lives, such as having been in care or homeless. We may assume that the challenges a student has in learning are because of a lack of schooling and not fully consider the combined impact and crossover effects of neurodiversity *and* adversity.

At the other end of the scale are those being missed as neurodivergent who are known as 'twice exceptional'. This is sometimes referred to as '2e' and has also been described as gifted students who have some form of disability. These are students with high levels of skills in specific areas such as maths, computing, sports or arts who also have neurodivergent traits. Their spiky profile may mean that the areas where they have comparative challenge may fall into what is considered the average academic range. This can result in their needs being missed or not considered as important enough by others for there to be an intervention. Once again, they miss being recognised as they are not considered 'bad enough' to require support and consequently do not receive the support they need to maximise their potential skills and talents.

KEY TAKEAWAYS

- Some students diverge from perceived social and cultural norms and do not gain support because their needs are missed, misdiagnosed and misunderstood.
- Bronfenbrenner's ecological systems theory is a useful framework to consider the varying and often complex interactions which can result in different outcomes for a child or adult.
- Service delivery models can vary in terms of how they operate and how diagnosis is made. Social inequity also makes a significant difference in identification.
- Intergenerational adversity can have a part to play in identification and gaining support. Parents of neurodivergent children may also be neurodivergent but not aware of this.
- Some students have challenges in gaining success in education because of cumulative adversity.
- There are many pathways to gain support or to miss out altogether in the identification of neurodivergent traits, and this may lead to significantly different outcomes and chances in education and in life.

4

MENTAL HEALTH AND WELLBEING

In this chapter we will consider:

- the theories and definitions relating to mental health and wellbeing;
- mental health and wellbeing in the context of neurodiversity;
- how our cognitive and hormonal development impacts who we are;
- some relevant theories about our 'selves' in the context of neurodiversity;
- what we can do to support all learners with their mental health and wellbeing.

MENTAL HEALTH AND PHYSICAL HEALTH

In our neurodiverse world, we all experience different, often fluctuating states of mental health and physical health. Throughout our lives, we may experience challenges with either or with both, sometimes simultaneously.

Often, it is easy to know if someone's physical health is not as good as it should be, or diverges from the norm, because it is visible to others. It is less easy to see if someone's mental health has altered or is directly impacting on their ability to function. And, because what goes on inside your head is usually hidden, mental illness can be hard for others to perceive, let alone comprehend. As Dean Burnett put it in his book, *Psycho-Logical* (2021): 'The human mind is far more flexible, variable and changeable than the human body. [...] It very rarely expresses itself in ways that show up under a microscope' (p. 37).

Difficulties with your physical state tend to attract more sympathy, perhaps because they appear easier to fix or support – you can, for example, have your arm in a plaster, be given a stick as an aid to walking, or benefit in the longer term from a wheelchair or prosthetic. From a medical perspective, curable physical illness usually follows a predictable pattern: confirmation, treatment, recovery, back to full functioning – using temporary or permanent aids if necessary.

Challenges with your mental health are, however, more often about adapting, coping, adjusting and managing. It may be much later in adulthood that you realise the impact of this and the toll it has taken on you throughout your life. Many people who have suppressed or not spoken of how they truly feel – perhaps because of their fear of labelling or the reactions of others – may only recently have become confident enough to open up and express themselves. People are increasingly talking about their mental health and want to understand more why we act and feel as we do.

Approaches to dealing with mental health challenges can involve quite elaborate and innovative workarounds, many of which remain private from others. These may include breathing exercises, 'wearing a mask' to fit in, or secret routines to make you feel brave enough to go to school or work in the morning. For many of us it is about learning to manage the brain we have been born with, and our reactions to the world and people around us, in a sustainable way.

Sometimes things that happen to us affect just our physical or mental health, but quite often they affect *both*. Having a physical injury can create significant pain and make us feel sad, depressed or uncertain about ourselves. Having problems with our mental health can lead to us being less physically active. A neurodivergent condition – which may further impact our mental or physical health negatively or positively – can make the picture more complicated, as we shall see later in this chapter.

Researchers are increasingly looking at what mental health and wellbeing might mean for neurodivergent learners. Richard Rose and colleagues in their paper, *Mental health and special educational needs: Exploring a complex relationship* (2009, p. 3), state that it can be hard to separate 'atypical behaviours [...] attributed to a diagnosed learning difficulty [from those] recognised as symptomatic of a mental health problem'.

The paper identified the need for clarification about the relationship between the two and for increased training opportunities to support teachers in their understanding of wellbeing theory and its practical applications. People know much more now about mental health and wellbeing than a decade ago, but there is still plenty to learn about how neurodivergent students are specifically impacted and how we can identify the root and extent of any challenges they may be facing.

WELLBEING

For many of us, what's going on with our mental health is closely linked to our *wellbeing*. According to the World Health Organization, wellbeing is about the extent to which we can cope with the normal stresses of life, work productively and contribute actively to our communities. In the most basic terms, wellbeing is about two things: how we *feel* and how we *function*.

How we *feel* is to do with how satisfied we are with life overall from our own, subjective point of view. It is about having a good balance of positive and negative emotions. A good balance means having much more of the former than the latter, but we must remember that none of us can feel good or happy all the time – we all experience challenges to our equilibrium at some point in our lives.

How we *function* is to do with our personal development. It is related to the extent to which we can engage in meaningful activities, have relationships with others and gain fulfilment in our lives. It is also about learning to accept both *who we are* and *what we could be* – concepts which are uppermost in many young people's minds but that remain with us all as we mature and evolve.

It is important to note as well that we can feel good but function badly, or feel bad but function well. Some individuals may be excellent at their roles – for example, top academics or athletes – and so appear always to be functioning at a high level. This could, however, mask the fact that they are struggling internally as a result of pressure, expectations, or having always to appear to be in good spirits. If we translate this into the school context, we can appreciate how A-grade or hyper-focused students – whether or not they are neurodivergent – may be camouflaging who they are or what they are feeling inside so that they fit into social norms, sometimes at great personal cost.

In her survey of the UK population at the beginning of this century, Felicia Huppert (2009) gave us a picture of the general state of the nation's mental health. If the same survey were carried out again today, the numbers may be different, especially because awareness of and conversation about mental health has considerably increased, but studies suggest a similar proportion of us – a minority – would have a mental health problem that requires medical intervention. We are yet to see the full impact of the Covid-19 pandemic on our mental health, but initial research, such as that carried out by Tami Benton and colleagues in 2021, suggests it has led to higher prevalence of clinically significant depression and anxiety symptoms in young people. This may be accentuated further for those who are neurodivergent and generally have higher rates of mental illness.

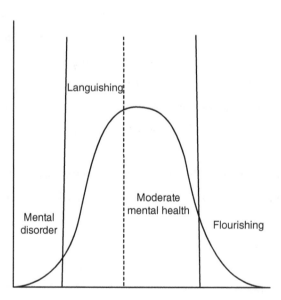

Figure 4.1   The mental health spectrum (adapted from Huppert, 2009)

In Figure 4.1, we can see that fewer than one in five people in Huppert's survey reported having some form of mental health problem, and a similar number were what was termed as 'flourishing'. This latter term is defined as referring to those who 'have enthusiasm for life and are actively and productively engaged with others and in social institutions' (Huppert, 2009, p. 137). Most of us were said to be somewhere in the middle, fluctuating between periods of feeling and functioning well.

COGNITIVE DEVELOPMENT

How we feel and how we function is, in part, a product of what is going on in our bodies. As we develop, our brains mature through what is known as synaptogenesis. This is about the creation of brain cells and the links between them, and their eventual 'pruning' to strengthen and remove connections according to how much they are used or how useful they are in our lives.

When considering cognitive development at a basic level, we should remember two things. First, our brains can't possibly retain and do everything, so pruning is a useful thing; and, second, our brains remain 'plastic' throughout our lives, meaning we can continue to adapt and take on new thoughts and ideas in adulthood, based on our experiences and our interactions with our environment and other people. A new context can also mean a new start. We will study the importance of this in learning in subsequent chapters.

It is helpful as well to appreciate the typical way our brains develop. Studies suggest that our visual cortex develops first, so that we can make sense early in our lives of what we see. The frontal cortex, which brain scans suggest is responsible for thinking, planning and self-control, develops and normally matures much later. This helps explain why adolescents may behave in ways that are hard for us to understand while they are in the often-difficult stage between childhood and adulthood. And again, there is no such thing as 'average'; we all evolve at different speeds.

Sarah-Jayne Blakemore and Uta Frith explain in *The Learning Brain* (2005) that there are critical periods in brain development requiring 'certain kinds of environmental stimulation at specific times [...] for the brain's sensory and motor systems to develop normally' (p. 25). It follows that the opportunity to learn certain things may be lost when we are children or adolescents.

In **Chapter 3** we underlined how not everyone starts from the same point in life or has the same opportunities. Misdiagnosis, missed diagnosis, misunderstandings, or lack of appropriate help at the right time can put individuals at a disadvantage from a young age. This can mean that those who are neurodivergent are always trying to catch up, make allowances for, or need additional support in activities that require certain levels of cognitive functioning. This will, in turn, impact on their mental health and wellbeing.

Similarly, there is evidence that there could be a delay in the emotional maturity of some young people who are neurodivergent. This could be related to delayed synaptogenesis or because they have had less opportunity to develop socially and emotionally.

HORMONAL DEVELOPMENT

Another aspect of how we develop concerns our hormones. A key element here is our hypothalamic–pituitary–adrenal (HPA) axis, which controls the relationship between the nervous and endocrine systems, deciding which chemicals go into your body, when they do so, and why. The axis is designed to be self-regulating but, increasingly, this is not always the case. This is thought to be due to the excessive stimuli we experience in today's world, such as through noise, light and digital devices.

If we are too stimulated – or stressed – too often, it can lead to an imbalance in how our brains function. We are no longer able to work out so easily when to take flight, fight, freeze, or simply get on with our lives because we are conditioned to be in a state of constant alert. 'Allostatic load' is the psychological term for the cumulative effect of stress and your body's response to stress over time. For some neurodivergent students, the load caused by their underlying genetics and the environment in which they are working can be overwhelming.

As we shall see in **Chapter 8** and **Chapter 9**, there are approaches we can use to control our reactions, but the more we are able to avoid, reduce or positively change anxiety-provoking situations or environments, the better. We should also remember that not all stress is bad: it can be motivating and support you in what you are aiming to achieve. Some people thrive on stress and actively seek it.

OUR SELVES

There is so much that we interact with in life that can make us feel and function well or not so well, and this can change over time. This last fact is important to communicate with young people who have less experience of life than you do.

HIERARCHY OF NEEDS

Many psychologists have written over the last century about our multidimensional needs. One of these was Abraham Maslow who, in the 1940s, defined his 'theory of human motivation'. He proposed that individuals have 'lower-order' needs that need to be met before you can access 'higher-order' needs, as shown in Figure 4.2.

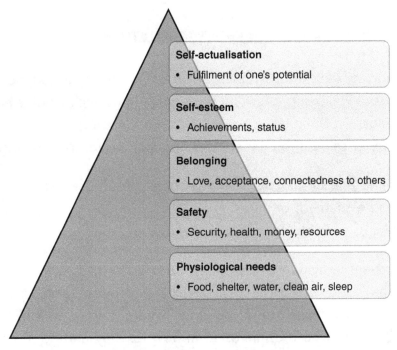

Figure 4.2   Maslow's hierarchy of needs

Research suggests that there is a significant correlation between academic success and having your lower-order needs met. In other words, if a student in your class is not getting enough food or exercise, or doesn't have a sup-portive friendship group, they may struggle to get good grades and meet targets in the subjects they are taking. Or, as has been suggested with refer-ence to another well-known taxonomy, you need to 'take care of Maslow before you can Bloom'.

Note, however, that in our neurodiverse world we may each have different perceptions of what it means, for example, to feel safe or belong. Many people can achieve and fulfil their potential without feeling connected to others or with comparatively poor health. Some people only seek self-actualisation and neglect other aspects of their lives.

It may in fact be more appropriate not to see the needs listed by Maslow as a hierarchy but as building blocks that may or may not be required. In **Chapter 8** we discuss as well whether Bloom's taxonomy is always appli-cable for those who are neurodivergent.

THEORIES OF SELF AND SELF-DETERMINATION

In her 'theory of self', the psychologist Carol Dweck suggested that learners' experiences of wellbeing at school have much to do with what is happening in their minds.

The theory of self can be understood through two forms of mindset:

1. perceiving oneself as comprising a collection of *fixed* traits to be meas-ured and evaluated; or
2. a system of malleable qualities *growing* over time.

Mindsets orient individuals to adopt diverse types of goals in educational settings. The 'fixed' mindset is typically adopted by learners who are inter-ested in *how well they are doing now*, whereas the 'growth' mindset is adopted by those who are interested in *how far they can go*. If you have a fixed mindset, you are more likely to believe in what is known as an 'external locus of control' – that how well you do is in the hands of others. If you have an 'internal locus of control' you feel that you have the power and responsibility for your propensity to learn.

These two belief patterns – the 'fixed' mindset and the 'growth' mindset – help explain how what you think can affect how you behave. Learners' mindsets can determine the type of goals they pursue, which together influence their performance at school and feed into how they feel about themselves. For example, some students who have fixed mindsets about their own intelligence may be more likely to experience negative emotions such as anger, anxiety, shame, helplessness and even boredom when learning, and typically perform less well in important schoolwork and assessments.

Alternatively, 'fixed' could refer to someone having an unshakable focus on a task, topic or goal to the exclusion of whatever else they could be doing. They may be 'growing' in one way but less so in others. Again, you may have in mind neurodivergent students who don't want to deviate from what they are doing because they are very clear on what they want to achieve and won't stop until they get there. To deny them this would mean they cannot reach self-esteem or actualisation. In this sense as well, their fixed mindset is related to their internal locus of control – they are self-motivated.

'Self-determination theory' is a theory on the *functional* side of wellbeing suggested by Richard Ryan and Edward Deci (2000), and one which has direct applicability in education. This theory suggests that individuals have three core psychological needs – competence, autonomy and relatedness – that, when fulfilled, result in higher wellbeing.

- *Competence* is about succeeding at activities we find challenging and being able to achieve the outcome we would like.
- *Autonomy* means experiencing freedom of choice and being in control of one's own actions.
- *Relatedness* refers to connectedness with others, feeling you can rely on others and that you and other people respect each other.

Education environments are generally set up in a good way for the first and third of these needs, but you may want to reflect on the extent to which learners can be autonomous in your educational environment. What could they achieve if they were given greater freedom in their studies, or if their learning were designed according to the principles of universal design (see **Chapter 5**)?

MENTAL HEALTH, PHYSICAL HEALTH AND NEURODIVERGENCE

Mental health conditions are common relating to some neurodivergent traits. Different neurodivergent traits are associated with different mental health conditions. We have set out some examples in Table 4.1.

Table 4.1   Mental health disorders and neurodivergent traits (adapted from Kirby & Cleaton, n.d.)

Condition	Anxiety	Mood	Obsessive-compulsive	Personality	Substance misuse
ADHD	X	X	X	X	X
ASC	X	X	X	X	X
DLD	X	X	X	X	
Dyslexia	X	X			
Tic disorders	X	X	X	X	

Neurodivergence can also be associated with negative psychosocial outcomes. 'Psychosocial' refers to the interaction between our thoughts and feelings and our social environment. It is important to remember, as with the disorders shown in Table 4.1, that not all neurodivergent individuals will experience these outcomes and that many experience positive outcomes from their neurodivergence, which they celebrate and makes them who they are.

In Table 4.2 you can find some examples of psychosocial outcomes commonly related to some neurodivergent traits. The challenge is understanding the interaction between the child and their environment and whether this is a result of or associated with these conditions. We know that children and young people with neurodivergent conditions are more at risk of mental illness and this is in part due to their daily experiences and challenges. Working hard to overcome barriers or screen out interference can take its toll and negatively impact on wellbeing, especially if the individual is continuously having to adapt and compensate.

Table 4.2 Examples of psychosocial outcomes in different neurodivergent conditions (adapted from Kirby & Cleaton, n.d.)

Outcome/ condition	Lower quality of life	Not in education, employment or training (NEET)	Poor academic achievement	Poor self- concept	Teenage pregnancy
ADHD	X	X	X		X
ASC	X			X	
DLD		X	X		X
Dyslexia	X			X	
Tic disorders	X		X	X	

We mentioned earlier in the chapter that your physical capacity at a given time can affect your wellbeing. If you have a neurodivergent condition that creates challenges for your movement, it may also impact on how you feel and function. For example, if you have DCD, not being able to play certain sports with other children can result in lower self-esteem and confidence. As we shall see in **Chapter 5**, educational environments have traditionally been designed to suit an 'average', so a student's place of study may be what interferes most with their ability to feel and function well.

Vincent Mancini's 'Environmental stress hypothesis' (Mancini et al., 2016) provides a schema for the many interacting factors contributing to why mental health conditions may not just co-occur with neurodivergent conditions but may be caused by them or by navigating the world as a neurodivergent person. If we take developmental coordination disorder (DCD) – also known as dyspraxia – as an example, we can see in Figure 4.3 how one thing can lead to another.

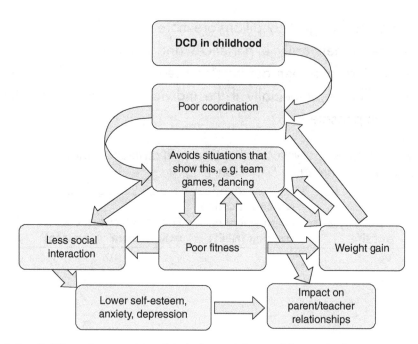

Figure 4.3 DCD and mental health (adapted from Kirby and Cleaton, n.d.)

You may like to consider the items in Figure 4.3 with reference to self-determination theory described above. What control, for example, do some individuals with DCD have over their interactions with others and their surroundings? Can a child with DCD join in with sport in school or are they regularly denied the opportunity? What additional challenges do their context and environment bring?

HOW CAN WE SUPPORT MENTAL HEALTH AND WELLBEING FOR ALL LEARNERS?

What we have described in this chapter reflects the biopsychosocial model suggested by George Engel (1979). As we saw in **Chapter 2**, this means that when we are supporting anyone with their mental health and wellbeing, we should consider it from the perspective of:

- biology – how our bodies work;
- psychology – how we think or understand;
- sociology – how the environment, events and relationships affect us.

Despite the often-hidden nature of mental health problems, teachers who are familiar with a group of students can usually spot when a student is not fully engaging. They might suddenly start misbehaving, getting behind in their work, playing truant, or become quieter. If we suspect something has changed, we can often find opportunities to talk to students in less formal ways and encourage them to reveal how they are feeling and why.

Whether or not we are able to distinguish between what can be attributed to a neurodevelopmental condition and a mental health problem, we can provide general support for how learners feel and function. This starts with encouraging an appropriate mindset, providing opportunities for healthy interactions with others and the environment, and suggesting different ways of approaching learning. As we shall see in **Chapter 8**, it can also be about taking responsibility for helping ourselves.

We might want to note as well how the Covid-19 pandemic opened new possibilities for some neurodivergent learners. Some may have made greater advances by studying at home than had they remained physically in their usual learning environment because they were away from distractions, able to focus better and had greater autonomy to divide up the day so that it felt more manageable for them. Those who already felt disconnected from school and their peers may have felt their wellbeing improved when they were learning remotely. Not being at school may have protected some students from bullying, social pressures or anxiety caused by interacting directly with others.

Learning at home will, of course, have brought a new set of challenges, as will learning online, but it may have given many neurodivergent children new opportunities. In terms of feeling and functioning, this is something that it would be a shame to lose.

KEY TAKEAWAYS

- Our mental and physical health fluctuate throughout our lives; how well we feel in our minds at a particular time is often hard for others to see or understand.
- Our wellbeing is to do with how we feel and how we function, which can be a product of our brain and hormonal development, and our interactions with the environment and other people, all of which are continually evolving.
- We can have different perceptions of the extent to which we feel each of our needs – such as safety, belonging and self-esteem – are or could be met.
- Poor mental health may be a result of a complex interaction between a student's environment and the student themselves, and this is often difficult to untangle.
- We can use a biopsychosocial approach to support others – and our ourselves – when we have challenges to our mental health and wellbeing.

5

REFRAMING

In this chapter we will consider:

- how special educational needs (SEN) labels can limit and skew our understanding of the lived experience of being neurodivergent;
- how shifting our focus from diagnosis and labelling to lived experience and impact on learning can help us to reframe our understanding of SEN;
- how we can draw on lessons from ecology to inform and shape the future of neurodiversity.

THE LIMITATIONS OF LABELS: A HISTORICAL LEGACY

In **Chapter 2** we outlined how we have made significant progress towards a better understanding of neurodivergence. However, progress is incremental and our current social and educational beliefs and practices are still shaped by what we previously believed. It is human nature to organise, categorise and label in order to make sense of the world around us, but the historical framing of neurodivergence linked to categorising and labelling has led to 'medical model thinking', which emphasises a deficit or problem within the individual that needs to be fixed (Naraian, 2019).

In the last few decades, there has been a much-needed shift from a narrower medical model towards more social model thinking. As discussed in

Chapter 2, the social model places emphasis on the *barriers* which undermine an individual's ability to access and participate fully in society. A wheelchair user only becomes disabled when a building is designed in a way which creates unnecessary barriers to access (e.g., steps rather than a ramp). In a similar way, when we provide a learner who finds the act of reading challenging with accessible materials (accessible font, colour background, etc.), the disabling barrier is significantly reduced or removed.

Because neurodivergence has long been associated with specialised professionals and often medicalised support, it has developed its own highly complex language, tools and systems. This frequently leads to teachers perceiving inclusive education as something that sits outside their remit or expertise. Similarly, parents or carers can be left feeling that they are out of their depth as they grapple with unfamiliar medical terminology or specialist language. Those without access to this specialised language can, through no fault of their own, be left with a somewhat surface-level understanding of neurodivergence. This can also influence an individual's understanding of their own diagnosis, even though it may feel incongruent with their lived experience.

WHAT'S IN A NAME? THE SHADOW OF A SEN LABEL

All words, terms or labels bring with them connotations, some of which are not accurate or indeed helpful. Nowhere is this more apparent than with regard to the language associated with labelling different SEN categories linked to neurodivergence. Even the terms 'SEN' and 'diagnosis' immediately conjure up images of support associated with remediation. Not only does the language associated with neurodivergence often reinforce medical model thinking, it also masks or blurs our understanding, which can lead to action which is also not always helpful.

Craig Collinson describes a 'shadow' which often accompanies a SEN label: a dominant perception based on a surface-level understanding of how a specific diagnosis might 'present', rather than accurately capturing an individual's lived experience (Collinson, 2012). For example, at face value, the terms 'attention deficit disorder' (ADD) and 'attention deficit hyperactivity disorder' (ADHD) indicate a shortfall or *deficit* in attendance. Yet the lived experience of those with ADHD or ADD is often not that that they *do not attend*, rather they *attend to everything* (Derrington, 2017, cited in University of Bath, 2018) (see Figure 5.1). The shadow perpetuates the notion that those with ADD/ADHD become easily distracted. Yet, if your brain attends to everything, it must then work much harder to avoid what are often interesting distractions.

This 'distraction' can take the form of external stimuli, where environmental factors compete for attention, or the individual's own thought processes, which can be hard to screen out. While the difference in terminology and interpretation may at first seem subtle, the translation of this into action is significant. This simple, but powerful reframing shifts our understanding from the label or presentation of a diagnosis to the lived experience which, in turn, will shape the strategies or interventions we put in place to support a learner.

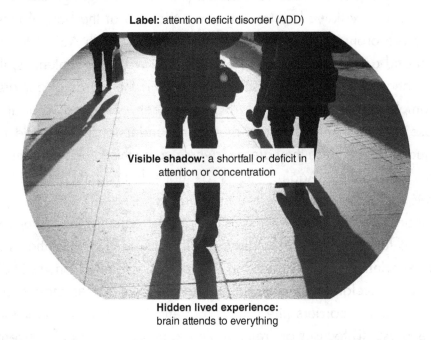

Label: attention deficit disorder (ADD)

Visible shadow: a shortfall or deficit in attention or concentration

Hidden lived experience:
brain attends to everything

Figure 5.1   Surface-level understanding of a label versus lived experience

In the same way, a common perception of autistic spectrum conditions (ASC) is based on the *presentation* of stereotypical traits associated with social communication, interaction and imagination (Wing, 2003). While these may be common features of ASC, this interpretation is limited to a surface-level understanding of what it means to live with an ASC diagnosis. Only recently has the definition of ASC been widened to recognise that many people with ASC experience hyper- or hypo-reactivity to sensory inputs such as having an adverse response to specific sounds or textures (American Psychiatric Association, 2013). Many individuals with ASC often have to work harder to channel out environmental factors which may remain unnoticed by others; noise, smells and even lighting can reduce functioning and make it harder to focus on communication, learning and the actions of day-to-day life.

ANALYSIS PARALYSIS

Many individuals with ASC may have heightened skills in analysis which, when not managed, can lead to 'analysis paralysis'. Language can represent a complex, highly flawed system of communication at the best of times; the more we are prone – as is often the case with those with ASC – to critique, question and analyse the meaning of individual words or sentences, the less able we become to express ourselves fluently via the words at our disposal. For example, some students with ASC have been paralysed when trying to compose an email, not because they can't understand the subtle nuance of language but because they are *overwhelmed* by this nuance and its accompanying possibilities. Again, this is a subtle but significant shift in our interpretation of the presentation of the barriers.

The shadow associated with specific labels frequently and inadvertently leads us to focus on the presentation of difficulties rather than the *lived and varied* experiences of the individual. Emphasis is placed on 'remediating' communication-related difficulties (the presentation) rather than managing the environmental barriers (the lived experience) for ASC. In the same way, the label of ADHD focuses on 'remediating' a perceived lack of concentration (presentation) rather than addressing environmental 'interference' (lived experience), as identified in Gallwey's formula.

The current model of assessment used for diagnosis of a condition also provides a static measure of achievement or skill. This may not always accurately capture or predict a learner's ability to develop beyond what has been measured at that moment in time. A diagnosis therefore provides limited value in terms of predicting future potential. If we allow this shadow to cloud our perception of a student's abilities, it can limit what we believe they are capable of. Indeed, many children with dyslexia, who may have struggled with mastering the skills associated with learning to read, will not necessarily go on to be poor readers in the future. Not only do we do a disservice to the students themselves, but we are at risk of potentially overlooking some of our brightest and most capable learners (Neuman & Roskos, 2005).

REFRAMING SEN: FROM DIAGNOSIS AND LABELLING TO LIVED EXPERIENCE AND IMPACT ON LEARNING

In the past we became preoccupied with the identification, diagnosis and labelling of neurodivergence linked to causes. If we now shift our perspective slightly, we can start to reframe our understanding and look beyond categorising causes to considering impact. The International Classification of Functioning (or ICF, World Health Organization, 2001), which we mentioned in **Chapter 1**, focuses on the relationship *between* the individual and their environment.

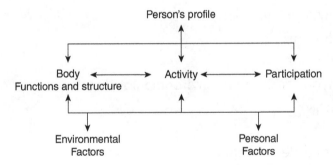

Figure 5.2   International Classification of Functioning (World Health Organization)

The ICF (see Figure 5.2) states that a person's level of functioning can change over time and is affected by a combination of factors, including their health, environment and other personal factors. This recognises therefore that a person's level of functioning is *fluid* rather than being fixed. This model helps us to consider the individual in relation to their environment. In turn, this reinforces the idea that the interaction between the individual and barriers they may face is in a constant state of flux.

Urie Bronfenbrenner's ecological systems theory (see Figure 2.2), which we referred to in previous chapters, helps us to take this thinking further and develop a more holistic approach to considering barriers across a range of contexts. We may experience barriers at a microsystem level (e.g., in the home or classroom), at a mesosystem level (within the local community), at an exosystem level (the media, parents, workplaces, friends or family) and the macrosystem level, linked to society's wider beliefs, values and customs.

As discussed in the **Introduction**, barriers to learning (and life in general beyond the classroom) can be understood in terms of the 'interference' such barriers create, which can ultimately undermine performance in education, the workplace and the wider community. We may find that the same barriers are frequently experienced in multiple contexts. The impact of the barrier might be lessened or exaggerated depending on the environment, but we will often be able to identify patterns linked to the barriers across a range of environmental contexts.

Here are some examples of common barriers which cause 'interference' across the individual's micro-, meso-, exo- and macrosystems:

- information/cognitive overload
- analysis paralysis
- working memory
- hyper- or hypo-sensitivity to environmental stimuli
- perfectionism
- anxiety
- low mood and demotivation.

The pattern associated with a barrier *across* different systems (micro, meso, etc.) provides an opportunity to gain a more holistic overview of the links between environment and the individual. Importantly, this means that the interventions and strategies we put in place can be transferable. For example, if an individual experiences interference from environmental stimuli in the home, understanding the pattern may enable us to understand and manage sensory interference across a range of other environments.

We can also learn from success in one context and use this to support the individual in other less familiar or more challenging contexts. For example, if a child uses a weighted blanket in the home environment to reduce anxiety, while a blanket may not be appropriate in the classroom, an alternative sensory input such as weighted wristbands may be effective.

THE FUTURE OF NEURODIVERSITY: LESSONS FROM ECOLOGY

In this chapter we have looked at the enduring legacy of SEN labelling, which continues to shape the way in which we interpret and make sense of neurodivergence. We would suggest that, rather than continuing to place emphasis on the need to identify and categorise learners with labels, we should instead 'reframe' our thinking around neurodiversity.

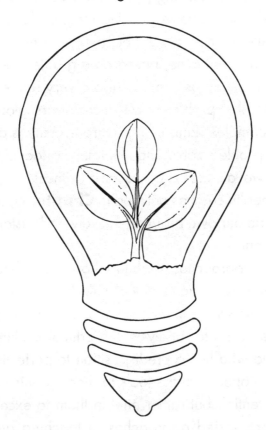

Figure 5.3   Harnessing the optimum conditions for each individual to thrive

Thomas Armstrong (2012) suggests that the human brain functions less like a computer and more like an ecosystem which needs to be nurtured rather than programmed. Reframing neurodiversity in this way helps us to better understand the link between an individual and their environmental context and how this can change over time. We can then create, adapt and harness the optimum conditions for each person to thrive educationally and beyond.

We are becoming acutely aware of the need to manage our global ecosystems in a way that is sustainable. In order to be truly impactful at addressing this goal, we also need to apply this thinking to people and in particular to the ways we all think, learn, work and live. When neurodiversity is upheld as a fundamental principle of education, we create the conditions for innovation, creativity and new ways of thinking (Hain et al., 2018). We therefore need to develop flexible and sustainable ways of learning, thinking and working which reduce or remove interference and enable people to meet their potential.

This is not simply a moral issue, based on a greater need for compassion; for the more cynical among us, there is also a very real ecological and economic incentive as the problems we face on a global scale become increasingly more complex. Embracing neurodiversity is about our ability to think differently, to problem solve and ultimately to identify creative solutions to the challenges we all face. As we also witness the emergence of an increasing mental health crisis as outlined in **Chapter 4**, understanding how to utilise and manage our own brains effectively and sustainably will become increasingly important.

With more varied approaches, a child who is considered to be disorganised can develop effective organisational skills by tailoring the tools they use to achieve this. A child who experiences analysis paralysis can be given the tools to harness their skills for analysis and critical thinking to find solutions to problems. A child who has a predisposition to perfectionism and anxiety can similarly be equipped with the tools to manage this in ways that do not undermine their potential, but rather enable them to excel. We will explore how to embed more varied approaches to teaching and learning in the classroom in **Chapters 8** and **9**.

KEY TAKEAWAYS

- Labels can limit and skew our understanding of neurodivergence as they can inadvertently lead to us focusing on the 'shadow' which often accompanies a SEN label.
- The historical framing of SEN has led to a focus on the *cause* of the barriers an individual may be experiencing rather than the *impact* of the barrier on learning, working and living.
- Reframing our thinking around neurodiversity leads to greater recognition of the importance of an individual's interaction with their environment and how this can fluctuate across a range of contexts and over time.
- Reframing also helps us move towards a more solution-focused approach where we use a range of flexible and adaptable interventions which work in a range of contexts.

6

UNIVERSAL DESIGN

In this chapter we will consider:

- how our current model of education, founded on principles from the industrial era, may not be adequately meeting the challenges to prepare all students for the future;
- how in our digital era we have the means to customise lessons, adapt formats of assessment and enable diverse types of students to have equitable access to the general curriculum;
- the anticipatory approaches we should take in order to be equitable and efficient, to designing educational settings instead of trying to retrofit our adjustments and support student by student;
- the concepts of universal design, and explore how we can use these approaches in different ways to meet the learning needs of all students.

EFFICIENCY, EQUALITY AND EQUITY

As we have read in previous chapters, we recognise that students engage in education in very different ways. In designing educational systems, we have perhaps tried for too long to deliver solutions to a mythical average learner. In secondary schools we generally operate on the assumption that most, if not all, students can read, write, spell, see and hear in the language of that country and that they can all be taught to complete the curriculum at the same pace, delivered in the same format.

The environment of the classroom is often a one-size-fits-all approach, despite students significantly varying in height and weight and around 11 per cent of students being left-handed. The length of lessons in a school time-table are also usually standard despite the reality that some students can only focus for ten minutes at a time. The standard lesson length is designed to accommodate the need for efficiency in the school rather than a learner's capacity to concentrate.

THE START OF DESIGNING FOR EFFICIENCY

The Industrial Revolution was a key point in manufacturing processes in Britain, continental Europe and the United States, between the middle of the 18th and 19th centuries. There was a move from hand-production methods to increasingly mechanised factory systems.

Over the next 100 years we started to see this approach influencing many other aspects of our lives. For example, in the 1940s we started to manufacture standardised furniture for homes, and it was a turning point for design which also used the concept of the mythical average man. Le Corbusier, the Swiss French architect, was one of the key proponents and developed his proportional system, known as 'Le Modulor'. When designing he was said to have had in mind a six-foot (1.8 metre) English policeman.

This standardised approach dictated the size and proportions of every-thing from the height of a door handle to the scale of a staircase. The average height of a woman in 2022 is 5 feet 4 in (1.65 metres), which means furniture or everyday items, such as kitchen cupboards and work surfaces which were designed for one size of person and not for all, are out of reach for many. The same approach also led to furniture in schools being designed without it reflecting or meeting the needs of many learners.

Is anyone really average? In the US in the 1980s, an experiment took ten different measures of 4,063 randomly selected males to try to decide what was the average man. The first of these measures was of standing height; out of the original sample of 4,063, only 1,055 – or 26 per cent – were found to be close to the average. When they added in all ten measures, they were left with no one who complied with all of them. William Bennett, a US paediatrician, showed that the growth charts that have been used to determine 'normal' weight and height are also based on many averages. Despite showing smooth growth curves, the reality is that child growth and development can vary hugely from one child to another and does not always progress in a linear fashion or at the same pace.

Furthermore, what is deemed as average also changes over time. The world's average person was described by *National Geographic* magazine in 2011 as being a right-handed Han Chinese male who spoke Mandarin. Despite 9 million men fitting this description in 2013, by 2030 the most 'typical' person will be a 26-year-old male from India, which demonstrates that our definition of an average person is socially constructed and is not static. What is neurotypical or average in a student is dependent on context and culture, as we have already discussed in **Chapter 2**.

STANDARDISED SCHOOLING

The large urban school, college, or university, organised by age stratification, with set numbers of students in each class, along with regulated units of time, was an excellent fit for the industrial era. Classrooms in the past were laid out to maximise floor space with instructors or teachers lecturing from raised platforms and pupils sitting at fixed desks many rows deep. Uniform delivery of services is efficient, with students organised in classes that meet on a regular basis at the same place at certain times of the day for a given length of time over a given period (a term or semester).

This predominant factory model of educational design remains our default model today. It is important to acknowledge that when planning large-scale education there is a need for standard approaches – especially when organising 100s and 1000s of students across a school day and year. Yet, it is also important to note that classrooms and an education system, which was predominantly designed for efficiencies of scale, will by its very nature, lead to many students experiencing increased barriers to learning and won't be fit for all.

MOVING FROM EQUALITY TO EQUITY

Delivering standard systems may result in equal delivery but certainly does not achieve *equity*. Despite a global fixation with standardisation in education, there are some prominent people over the last century who have fought against it. One such person was the Italian physician Maria Montessori who recognised the need for creating spaces that varied depending on the size and development of the child. In 1900, she was the co-director of the *Scuola Magistrale Ortofrenica* in Milan, which was a 'medico-pedagogical institute', with an attached laboratory classroom, for training teachers in educating 'mentally disabled children' (this was the wording of the time).

During her two years at the school, Montessori developed methods and materials which she later adapted to use with mainstream children. She created spaces in the classroom to encourage children to move around in the lessons and replaced the heavy standard furniture with child-sized tables and chairs light enough for the children to move. She also placed child-sized materials on low, accessible shelves. She included activities for students to care for their environment and their selves, including flower arranging, hand washing, gymnastics, care of pets and cooking.

In the US in the 1960s and 1970s the rigid and standardised approaches were also challenged in some schools with the introduction of open-education classrooms, free of walls, and students grouped by subject matter and skill. Teachers moved freely from class to class. They were attempting solutions to the question of how to get the school environment right for different children – although, of course, such open-plan approaches don't work for all.

Another person who continues to have a significant impact on educational design globally is Reuven Feuerstein, an Israeli clinical, developmental and cognitive psychologist, who worked with children from across the world who had been subject to trauma or who were profoundly disabled. Feuerstein, like Montessori, recognised the importance of modifying the environment, and developing students' cognitive functions and metacognitive skills.

Feuerstein emphasised the need to create meaningful learning environments where children can realise their potential. He also saw that the assessment process could be the beginning of positive change for students if they and their teacher considered what the outcomes really meant.

MOVING TOWARDS EQUITY: CONSIDERING UNIVERSAL DESIGN

The concept of universal design (UD) shapes an environment so that it can be accessed, understood and used by as many people as possible by all, regardless of age, size, or cognitive or physical abilities.

In Figure 6.1 you can see the three important components of universal design:

- *usability* – we need processes and practices that are simple and intuitive for every person to use;
- *accessibility* – this is about being equitable, meaning that not everyone receives the same thing;
- *inclusion* – for this we need to take a proactive approach, so that everyone can integrate and participate in current systems.

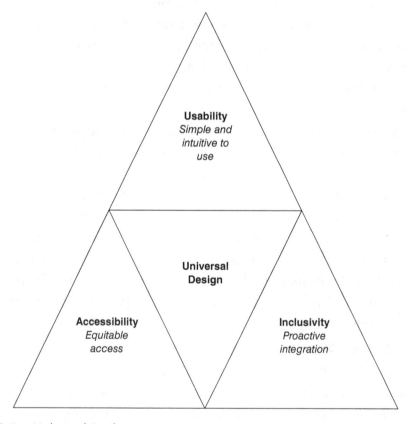

Figure 6.1   Universal Design

The principles of UD consider that an environment (such as a building, product or service in that environment) should be designed to meet the needs of all people who wish to use it.

Even if you are not familiar with the term 'universal design', you have likely encountered it in your everyday life. Today we recognise that to be accessible a building needs to have lifts as well as stairs. We can now speak into some devices to record or request information rather than having to press buttons. To be successful, design principles need to be thought of at the *start* of a process. Retrofitting is often expensive and takes time and cost to implement.

In the context of education, ensuring that learning is accessible for all when we design it means that we shouldn't need to make adjustments for students on an individual basis. An example of this could be ensuring that information is accessible for students when they are reading, listening, or following instructions. If the information is delivered in multiple formats such as audio, video or with static pictures, we can reach more students immediately, rather than reviewing what each student requires one at a time.

WHAT IS THE UDL FRAMEWORK?

Universal design for learning (UDL) takes the principles of UD a step further. UDL is an anticipatory approach to teaching and learning that gives all students the opportunity to succeed. UDL is not about finding one way to teach all students but takes the opposite approach. The goal of UDL is to use a variety of teaching methods to remove any interferences or barriers to learning and optimise potential.

UDL is a useful framework for developing lesson plans, activities, resources and assessments. It can be used across multiple aspects of teaching and learning, design and delivery. It is based on three main principles (see Figure 6.2).

The three key components of UDL describe:

1. *The Why (engagement) – how can we motivate students and sustain their interest?*

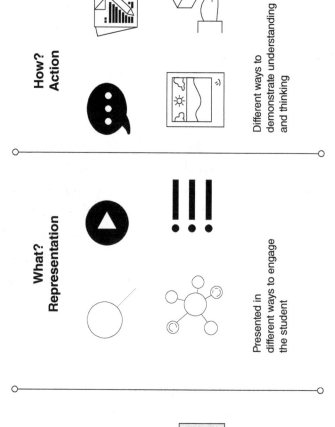

Figure 6.2 Universal design for learning

For example:

- find out what interests the students and use this to teach other topic areas and extend their learning;
- give assignments that feel relevant to students' lives, including their culture;
- gamification – allow students to work at their own pace and encourage them to extend their skills by improving on their own outcomes;
- provide clear aims and objectives so the student knows why they are doing the work and what the expected outcome is going to be;
- understand the motivation of the student to engage.

2. *The What (representation) – providing information in different formats.*

For example, the teacher could provide class notes and:

- an audio transcript of a lesson the student can listen to after the lesson;
- a video that could be replayed multiple times for or by the student so they can rewatch the steps that have been demonstrated in class;
- hands-on opportunities to learn and practise a new skill.

3. *The How (action and expression) – how will the student demonstrate learning and understanding to others and for themselves?*

For example, understanding could be demonstrated in different ways such as:

- completing a written task;
- giving an oral report;
- making a video or a comic strip;
- doing a group project.

UDL is not an approach to teaching or to workplace training that specifically targets people who are neurodivergent but can be particularly helpful for *any* student who needs adaptations to tasks and environments to be able to engage and participate actively and feel comfortable doing so. UDL asks us to expand our concept of both *where* learning can take place and *what* needs to be available for learning to take place. UDL is not a fixed manual with set processes but a guide describing ways to consider flexible solutions that help provide access for all students.

Moving from an industrial era to a digital era, the ability to put in place a range of different ways to deliver education is one of the key drivers for UDL. In addition to this, we recognise the importance of gaining digital skills to navigate the world of work. We have moved from the industrial era of standardisation to the digital era of personalisation (see Table 6.1).

Table 6.1 Industrial era vs digital era

Industrial era	Digital era
Taught to	Learn with
Directed learner	Flipped classroom and facilitated learning
Knowledge defined	Knowledge discovered
Explicit knowledge	New and developing knowledge
Single assessment process: 'high stakes'	Multiple assessment processes in different formats and in different times, including gamification
Focus on reading, writing and arithmetic	Recognition of variable cognitive routes to learning and need for digital and emotional skills
Teacher-led	Collaborative learning across ages and skills and professions
Single learners	Learning from and with each other
Content learning	Critical reflection, communication, design and exploration
Linear learning process	Variable routes within learning
Fixed environment	Variable settings for learning

The pandemic has shone a spotlight on the need for us to get better at personalising and tailoring learning. We have seen sudden changes in the delivery of education that have meant students and teachers have had to adapt quickly. For example, the idea of the 'flipped classroom', which has been debated for well over a decade, came alive during this time. A flipped classroom refers to learning where students are introduced to learning materials at home in advance of the lesson and the teacher takes on a facilitative role in class to consolidate their learning.

Technology also expanded the range of ways to engage that we could not previously have considered. Students can now participate in discussions using closed captioning, 'chat' and 'hands-up' functions. Digital technology enables us to repurpose or reformat flexible resources to meet the needs of everyone.

As you can see in Table 6.1, there are some key tools and aspects of the digital era that particularly benefit some neurodivergent students. Many benefitted from being at home during the pandemic as it was quieter, with less external sensory stimuli (e.g., noisy children). For some students they were more in control of when and where they could learn. They could choose to record information on their computer rather than by handwriting. Such an experience makes us think about different settings and potential interferences to learning and how modifying the environment can increase or decrease both engagement and emotional wellbeing.

FROM THE DESIGN OF BUILDINGS TO THE DESIGN OF LEARNING

We've progressed from designing for the average to being able to adapt our environments in ways that we could not conceptualise or deliver in the industrial era. We have the potential for even greater personalisation. However, while we have started to make great strides in applying the principles of universal design to ensure better access to buildings and the tools we use to support learning, such as adaptive furniture and software, we still need to apply this approach more systematically to the actual 'building blocks' of teaching and learning.

Universal design helps us to anticipate and plan for learning activities, resources and assessments which are no longer designed for a mythical 'average' student. Instead, if we design teaching and learning to cater for those students who are at greater risk of existing at the margins of the educational system, we actually find that the overall effectiveness of learning increases for all students. By considering universal design we move away from 'othering' specific groups and create the right physical and cognitive conditions for everyone to thrive. In the next chapter we will discuss how we can draw on the principles of universal design to embed practical and transferable inclusive practices in the classroom.

KEY TAKEAWAYS

- By using the principles of universal design we can meet the needs of more students.
- Universal design for learning (UDL) helps us to deliver teaching and learning which anticipates students' needs and plans for this at the point of design, rather than having to make bolt-on adjustments.
- UDL enables us to make improvements for all learners: by designing in a way that meets the needs of those students who may traditionally have been marginalised in the education system, we make learning more effective and efficient for all students.
- Recognising that we learn at different paces and need different approaches is fundamental to the success of UDL.

7

THE INCLUSIVE CLASSROOM

In this chapter we will consider:

- how we can work as teachers and educational professionals to recognise and harness the neurodiversity of the learners in our classrooms so that all our learners can thrive;
- practical steps which busy and often overworked teachers can take to develop inclusive practice in a way that is manageable and sustainable.

GETTING STARTED

In the previous chapter we discussed universal design and how its principles can be used in the classroom to help all learners succeed. In this chapter we will demonstrate how embedding inclusive practice in response to the needs of those at the margins can boost the overall effectiveness of learning for everyone and reduce the need for teachers to make individual adjustments – thus saving the busy teacher much-needed time and energy.

Although many teachers are committed to the idea of inclusive education, they can feel overwhelmed and ill-equipped to do this while juggling the varied demands of a busy classroom (Ross, 2017). It is important to remember that great inclusive teaching and learning does not look that different from great teaching and learning in general; many teachers are often already using inclusive approaches without identifying them as such or recognising that they are doing so.

Before we begin exploring how to develop a practical and sustainable approach to meeting the needs of multiple learners, it can be useful to consider what we actually mean when we talk about inclusivity. The term 'inclusive' can be hard to pin down, particularly in terms of what it looks like in practice in the classroom.

The inclusive classroom approach (see Figure 7.1) helps to remind us that, in order truly to support and harness everyone's talents, we should not only give *access* to all students in the physical sense but also enable them to *participate* fully in the learning experience and *progress* their learning in order to meet their full potential.

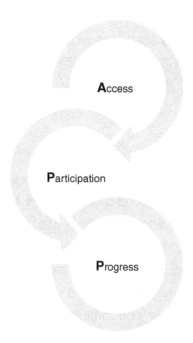

Figure 7.1   The inclusive classroom

Embedding inclusive practices in the classroom represents a process. This can be done over a period of time by making small adaptations and then evaluating the impact on learning of such changes. This approach is often used to make marginal improvements in many sports, such as cycling. A few simple changes are likely to be more effective than trying to change everything in one go. It is important to start small and build confidence and skills gradually.

In this chapter we have broken down this process into a number of practical and achievable steps which will help the busy teacher engage in inclusive practice in a way that is as meaningful and impactful as possible. Here are a series of steps that we can take to remove barriers to learning. Rather than seeing this as a process that you engage in only once, think of it as a cycle you can repeat multiple times.

1. Identify a range of barriers to learning across the student cohort (using the patterns beyond labels model, which we will describe below).
2. Focus on the impact of the barrier on learning and the 'interference' it may generate, rather than the cause associated with a specific label.
3. Work with students to introduce strategies to remove, reduce and/or rethink the impact of the barrier. Embed these within your whole-class teaching sessions, learning activities and assessments.
4. Work with the students to evaluate the impact of the strategy on removing the barrier and make any necessary adjustments.
5. Work with students and colleagues to transfer and apply the most impactful strategies to other contexts within and beyond the classroom.

It is important to note that the approach we outline is not intended to replace the need for specialised one-to-one support or invaluable provision from other professional services such as additional learning support, pastoral care or access to special exam arrangements. Instead, we outline a practical approach to embedding inclusive practice in the classroom which can be used in addition to signposting students to extra support to which they may be entitled.

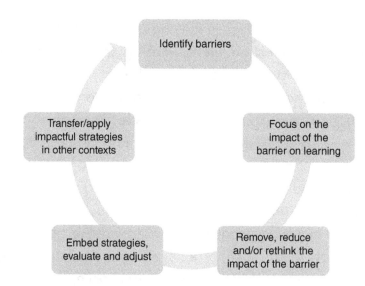

Figure 7.2   Five-step cycle to impactful inclusive practice

STEP 1: IDENTIFYING PATTERNS BEYOND LABELS

'Patterns beyond labels' (Eaton and Osborne, 2019) is a model which helps teachers to support their students in a way that is sustainable but is also impactful in delivering the inclusive classroom approach (access, participation, progress). While supporting individual student need is an effective approach when working on a one-to-one or small group basis, it can be more challenging for the teacher when supporting an entire class with potentially very different needs.

The model encourages us to look at patterns of challenge or barriers to learning which exist *across* the student cohort. If we shift our perspective away from individual labels and instead consider impact on learning, we can identify common patterns in barriers to learning. For example, instead of focusing on the 'differences' between a dyslexia or ADHD label, we can support students to manage interferences which might undermine their ability to concentrate and learn effectively.

Such an approach enables us, above all, to reach those learners who haven't met the threshold to get a diagnosis. In **Chapter 3**, we discussed how a large number of students may have been missed, misdiagnosed or had their needs misunderstood (the 3 Ms). We emphasised the importance of meeting and understanding students' different needs and presentations within the classroom.

Many of the challenges that our neurodivergent students face are not distinctly different to the challenges we *all* face, but just tend to be more exaggerated. The strategies which support neurodivergent students will better enable *all* students to fulfil their potential. For example, strategies such as breaking down tasks into small steps, or the use of visuals to support memory, are meaningful strategies which support all learners (DANDA, cited in Colley, 2006).

The patterns beyond labels model (see Figure 7.3) consists of three lenses – physical, cultural and cognitive – which can be used to help us think about the different types of barriers our students may face. By focusing on the three lenses, we ensure that we are working towards enabling equitable access, participation and progress as identified by the inclusive classroom approach.

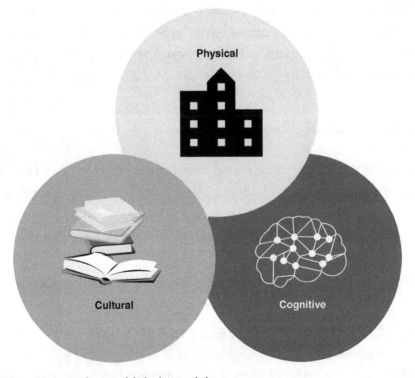

Figure 7.3   Patterns beyond labels model

THE PHYSICAL LENS

The physical lens focuses on the teaching and learning environment or *where* learning takes place. It enables us to think about access to both the physical environment such as a building, classroom or playground (and toilets and changing spaces), as well as the physical resources we provide. It also includes access to digital learning spaces and resources. This tends to be the lens that is most associated with ensuring inclusion and increasing accessibility.

THE CULTURAL LENS

The cultural lens helps us to focus on the *what* of learning. It enables us to consider the relevance of the examples and resources we use to effectively engage a diverse student cohort. The cultural lens also helps us to make explicit those aspects of teaching and learning which can sometimes remain hidden to students, such as the importance of teachers providing clear and explicit guidance and not making assumptions about what students know. It asks us to consider the need for cultural adaptation and be sensitive to the differences in understanding and beliefs within the communities where we work.

THE COGNITIVE LENS

The cognitive lens encourages us to consider *how* students learn. It focuses on the nuts and bolts of teaching and learning: how students process, assimilate, organise, recall and synthesise information. It enables us to facilitate flexible modes of teaching delivery, and to build in choice and flexibility when designing learning activities and assessments. It also encourages us to explore metacognitive strategies with our learners, which we will describe in more detail in **Chapter 8**.

A HOLISTIC APPROACH TO DEVELOPING INCLUSIVE PRACTICE

While the lenses can be used in isolation, they are most effective and impactful when used in conjunction to consider how a barrier may undermine a student's learning potential. For example, we tend to think of access to a classroom primarily in physical terms (as supported by the physical lens): we might consider barriers associated with mobility or wheelchair access.

If we then draw on the cognitive lens in conjunction with the physical lens, we can start to apply a more nuanced approach to considering how our environment may influence and impact on the learning experience. Some neurodivergent learners may, for example, experience either heightened or reduced awareness to sensory triggers such as light, noise or certain textures. Using the lenses in this way helps us to reframe how we view potential barriers or sources of interference and promotes a more holistic approach to inclusive practice.

STEP 2: HOW TO INTERPRET 'INTERFERENCE' AND ITS UNDERMINING IMPACT ON LEARNING POTENTIAL

As teachers, our ability to observe, interpret and make accurate judgements is fundamental and one of our greatest assets. In a busy classroom, this is not always easy as we must grapple with multiple forms of 'interference' as well. In addition, some of the most familiar tools we rely on in the classroom to help us make these observations and judgements don't always facilitate a meaningful interpretation of what we are observing; indeed, they can inadvertently reinforce Collinson's shadow, as mentioned in **Chapter 5**.

Bloom's taxonomy of learning (see Figure 7.4) is one of the most influential learning theories of the past few decades and has shaped many aspects of everyday teaching practice. Bloom's taxonomy provides a useful tool for thinking about types of cognition and how this links to learning activities, assessments and learning outcomes. However, because the taxonomy is often presented in the form of a hierarchy, it can inadvertently skew our perception of student ability or potential, particularly regarding neurodiversity.

The arrangement of the hierarchy has led to the frequent perception that the skills are ordered in terms of complexity as we move from the bottom to the top of the hierarchy. Consequently, we often correlate the different levels of skill with the distinct stages of a student's educational journey – the skills at the bottom of the hierarchy are primarily associated with early years education and a student is seen to progress towards the higher-level skills as they move into secondary school, further education and beyond.

One of the challenges of the hierarchy is that it can lead us to assume that if a student finds the skills at the bottom of the hierarchy difficult to master, then they will be less likely to progress and develop those skills further up the hierarchy. The context of neurodiversity can help us to reframe Bloom's taxonomy and rethink the observations and assessments we make regarding learners' educational potential.

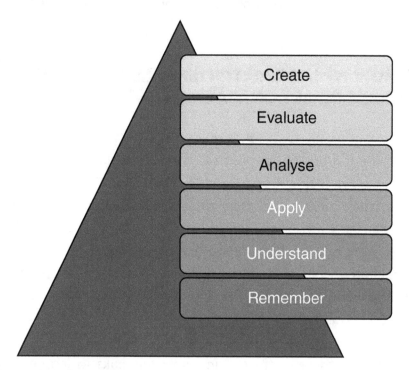

Figure 7.4   Bloom's taxonomy

Let's take the example of a simple classroom exercise where the students are asked to sort and categorise a muddled assortment of cutlery. On the face of it, this seems like a very simple task and would enable us to assess the students' ability to describe, categorise and organise. Imagine that we observe a student who appears unable to complete the task. If they are experiencing barriers when employing foundational level skills, we could quite easily assume that this student will therefore struggle to master skills that appear further up the hierarchy. And this is where a better understanding of neurodivergence can help us to reframe our observations and challenge our assumptions.

We could presume that most students would identify the more obvious features or characteristics by which to organise the cutlery such as by type. For some neurodivergent learners, their difficulty in completing the task may in fact be due to them possessing skills towards the top of the hierarchy. If an individual has a heightened ability to analyse and can see detail and therefore numerous ways of potentially sorting the cutlery, this could undermine their ability to complete the task in the way we are expecting students to do it. The individual might notice size, shape, texture or patterns on the cutlery, making the task of systemically sorting and organising it much more of a challenge for them. In this example, it is the student's heightened skill set towards the top of the hierarchy which is actually undermining their ability to complete seemingly more simple tasks that we might associate with the cognitive skills towards the bottom of the hierarchy.

THE PARADOX OF ANALYSIS PARALYSIS

Reframing Bloom's taxonomy in this way enables us to see links between different types of cognition. Heightened skills in analysis, evaluation and synthesis (when not managed) may lead to potential information overload and what is referred to as 'analysis paralysis', where the student feels unable to make a decision or commit to a single course of action because they simply see too many possibilities and make too many links (see **Chapter 5**).

Again, this helps us to move beyond a label and its presentation and encourages us instead to manage the lived experience of the individual student. We can see how this is impacting on educational performance and, in turn, directly shape and influence the strategies or interventions we put in place for the learner. In this example, clear and explicit instructions and strategies which scaffold and manage the potential for analysis paralysis will better enable the learner to carry out the task.

STEP 3: THE 3 Rs: REMOVING, REDUCING AND RETHINKING BARRIERS TO LEARNING

Once we have identified patterns in the barriers to learning our student cohort might face, we can use the '3 Rs' (Osborne, 2021) to help us remove, reduce and rethink the interference such barriers might present (see Figure 7.5). The 3 Rs help us to develop a solution-focused approach to overcoming barriers, whether this is in the classroom, the workplace or even in the home. We have supplemented these with a fourth R, *reflect*, to represent a good starting point prior to considering the 3 Rs.

Figure 7.5   The 4 Rs

REFLECT

Once we have identified a potential barrier to learning, the *reflect* prompt encourages us to consider how we might work best with the learner to help them overcome the barrier. The following Rs of 'remove', 'reduce' and 'rethink' provide different ways forward in managing and overcoming sources of potential interference.

REMOVE

The *remove* prompt enables us to consider whether we can take away a potential barrier or hurdle which is preventing a student from fulfilling their potential. In an education context, this might include removing a barrier associated with a particular form of assessment so that a student can meet the learning outcomes in a way that is accessible to them. For example, if a student finds presenting particularly challenging, but this is not specifically contained within the learning outcomes, then you could consider using an alternative form of assessment which enables the student to meet the assessment criteria, such as producing a poster or video presentation. We will consider this in more detail, regarding validity and fairness, in **Chapter 9**.

REDUCE

Reduce encourages us to explore whether the impact of the barrier could be reduced or minimised. For example, if presenting is a required and necessary feature of the assessment and learning outcomes, then we might be able to consider whether we could build flexibility into the assessment mode itself. This might include enabling a student to present to a smaller group or to produce a recording of their presentation.

RETHINK

The final R encourages us to think creatively about how to support the student to overcome the hurdle. If we take again the same example of presenting, this is an important skill and, as teachers, we should be providing students with a rich and truly inclusive educational experience. Simply removing a hurdle does not always enable the student to participate fully and could impact on the student's progress in the long run. *Rethinking* the nature of the interference the barrier creates helps us to work with the student to find strategies or approaches which will enable them to overcome the barrier in a way that is manageable and sustainable. This could include setting a longer-term goal for the student so they can practise the skill over a prolonged period, or may mean exploring a range of interventions which target the specific challenges they are facing linked to presenting, whether this is to do with supporting working memory, challenges associated with communication or increased anxiety.

STEP 4: EMBED, EVALUATE AND ADJUST

Once we have identified potential strategies which can help to remove, reduce, or rethink barriers, these can then be *embedded* in the classroom – again remember that this can be a gradual process and will work best when interventions are brought in at a pace that does not overwhelm the student (or teacher!). When thinking about how to embed strategies or interventions it can be useful to consider how both the teacher *and* student can work together to implement effective interventions. This will involve considering what the teacher can do at the point of teaching design and delivery and what the student can do to adapt their experience of learning.

While the role of the teacher is fundamental in shaping and embedding effective inclusive practice, we must not overlook the importance of equipping students with the tools to adapt their own learning experiences. At its most effective, inclusive education becomes a shared space between teachers and their students. Emphasising this aspect of inclusive teaching and learning not only leads to impactful inclusive practice but also practice that is sustainable for the teacher and an active approach to learning for the students.

We have separated inclusive teaching *and* inclusive learning into two halves. In reality, the two overlap as teachers and learners take joint ownership of the learning process, but it can be helpful to distinguish between the two interlinking halves: those adaptations teachers can make and those which students can make (with a teacher's support and the right scaffolds in place) – see Figure 7.6. Both are made in response to the needs of each student. We will explore practical examples of both teacher-led and student-led strategies which support inclusive teaching and inclusive learning in the following chapter.

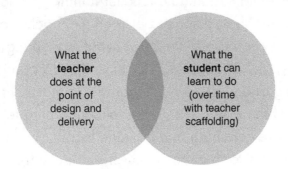

Figure 7.6   Teacher-led adaptations and student-led adaptations

WHAT THE TEACHER DOES AT THE POINT OF DESIGN OR DELIVERY

This is the approach which is promoted via universal design for learning as discussed in **Chapter 6**. It involves building in choice and flexibility at the design and delivery stage of teaching in terms of how students engage with their learning and how they demonstrate their learning via assessment (CAST, 2020). This could include using a range of assessment types or building in choice in terms of topic for a learning activity.

WHAT THE STUDENT CAN LEARN TO DO (OVER TIME, PROMPTED AND SCAFFOLDED BY THE TEACHER)

While it is important for teachers to make adaptations to their teaching instruction in response to learners' needs, students can also devise adaptations for flexible and autonomous learning. Supporting students to adapt their own learning in this way not only boosts motivation and learner auton-omy but can also help them to see how the strategies can be transferred to multiple contexts beyond the classroom. For example, if a student finds a planning table supports their thinking and writing better than the more com-monly used mind map (which can lead to analysis paralysis!), they may then find this same technique, when adapted, works in multiple contexts across different subjects and types of task. This in turn helps students to consolidate their learning and build sustainable long-term thinking and learning habits.

Fundamental to this shared space between the teacher and their students is the need to review on a regular basis what is working and what is not. When embedding inclusive strategies, remember to regularly *evaluate* the impact on learning and work with the learners to make changes to improve the effectiveness of the approach. In the following chapter, we will explore the role of facilitative coaching and how the teacher can use this approach to encourage learners to think for themselves and reflect on what may or may not be working and why. This is fundamental as you may find that a strategy which works well on one day in a specific context may need adapting in order to be impactful at or in a different time, situation or environment. This doesn't have to be a major change; sometimes minor, carefully considered tweaks may increase the effectiveness of a particular approach.

STEP 5: TRANSFERRING IMPACTFUL STRATEGIES TO MULTIPLE CONTEXTS WITHIN THE CLASSROOM AND THE SCHOOL

As mentioned at the start of the chapter, we can quickly feel overwhelmed if we focus on the many things we could be doing to make our classrooms more inclusive. Rather than focusing on lots of separate strategies for different areas of teaching practice, it can be useful to consider how we can *transfer* ways of thinking across different areas of the subject and school curriculum. Instead of generating potential lists of actions or steps for separate areas of practice, try to consider how an effective strategy you are using could be applied across the range of teaching and learning-related practices including your teaching delivery, learning activities, resources and assessment (see Figure 7.7).

As an example, you may find using images to support the use of verbal or written instructions (which we will explore in **Chapter 8**) is a useful approach you can use when preparing your teaching delivery. The same approach can be transferred and used to support the design of your learning activities, the resources and in-class assessments you create.

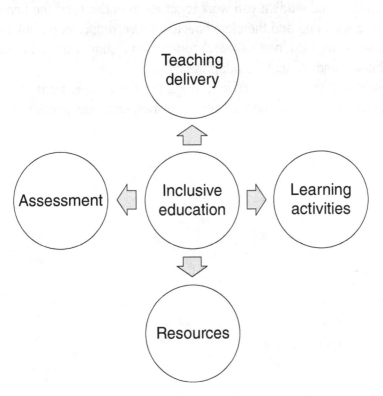

Figure 7.7   Transfer of inclusive strategies to all four areas of the curriculum

In this chapter we have introduced a number of approaches to help you develop your inclusive classroom and harness all students' neurodiverse skills. The five-step cycle introduces a practical method the busy teacher can use to bring about meaningful, sustainable and impactful change. Remember that developing inclusive practice is a process and one that can be developed over time.

KEY TAKEAWAYS

- The process of developing the inclusive classroom can be broken down into several manageable steps which enable the busy teacher to develop their practice over time. This approach will ensure that educational access, participation and progress all improve.
- The teacher can look for patterns in barriers across the cohort which undermine learning potential using physical, cultural and cognitive lenses.
- The teacher and student can work together to understand the impact of the barrier on learning and therefore how to remove, reduce or rethink the barrier.
- The teacher and students can work together in a shared space to embed both teacher-led and student-led adaptations.
- Teachers can 'transfer' effective strategies to the various areas of their teaching practice, including their delivery, activities, resources and assessments.

8

TEACHING AND LEARNING

In this chapter we will consider how to:

- manage the learning environment for neurodivergent students;
- manage our communication as teachers so that students can fully access and make use of the knowledge we present to them;
- help students to explore their own metacognition at a more nuanced level;
- put wellbeing at the heart of teaching and learning, rather than positioning it as a bolt-on provision which exists outside the classroom;
- draw on coaching techniques to help our students to develop and grow;
- transfer and embed effective and impactful inclusive teaching and learning strategies across our teaching practice, as well as in a range of contexts beyond the classroom.

At its most effective, inclusive education involves both the teacher and students working together to embed practices which promote inclusive teaching *and* inclusive learning. In this chapter we will explore a range of general approaches which teachers and students can implement to embed inclusive teaching and learning effectively. As in any cycle of reflective practice in education, teachers and students should decide which approaches are the best fit for their context, try them out, evaluate and adapt them so that they are as effective and impactful as possible.

It is important to note that the approaches we share in this chapter are *not* designed to replace the need for specialised one-to-one support delivered by trained professionals. Instead, you can use the approaches to facilitate and harness learner neurodiversity in the classroom, helping those students who are most in need of support, as well as those students who may not have met the required threshold for a diagnosis. And you can use the approaches to help *all* students to reflect on and refine their learning to nurture a community of resilient and autonomous learners.

While this chapter introduces some general teaching and learning approaches to inclusive practice in response to common challenges, remember also to draw on your own expertise and knowledge of *your own* student cohort, subject discipline and local context (Haug, 2017) (see Figure 8.1). This is fundamental in ensuring the success of the approaches you choose. Use the 'patterns beyond labels' model to identify what is most relevant to your students, your teaching and your school.

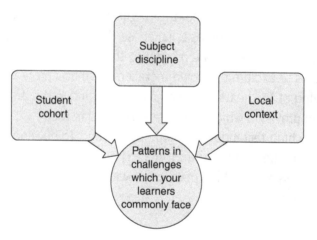

Figure 8.1   Identifying patterns of need linked to local context

MANAGING THE ENVIRONMENT TO SUPPORT COGNITIVE AS WELL AS PHYSICAL COMFORT

We often consider inclusive education in terms of how the physical environment can create barriers to learning. However, it is important to consider the *sensory environment* as well as physical accessibility, particularly when understanding that our senses directly influence our cognitive functioning and wellbeing. Factors such as light, noise, smell or the ability to move can impact both positively and negatively on our concentration, focus and motivation.

It can be useful for us as teachers to consider how our classroom environment may cause interference that undermines the learning potential of some of our students, especially for some neurodivergent learners where specific sensory triggers can impact on their emotional wellbeing. We can take this into account when arranging the classroom, designing learning activities and carrying out assessments. In addition to considering this and making possible adaptations to the learning environment, we can equip our learners themselves to interact with the environment in a way which supports their cognition.

It can be helpful to rethink barriers which might be linked to a perceived and normalised 'ideal' of what a learning environment should look like. We may assume that learning in silence, at a clear and tidy desk, with bright lighting and a chair which supports good posture provides the ideal learning conditions; but while the science of ergonomics may suggest that this is physically accurate, it is not always true when we consider our 'cognitive' comfort (Osborne et al., forthcoming 2023). When writing this book, we all adapted our environment to 'boost' our ability to think and write, drawing on our own preferences and needs, to create tailored versions of our 'ideal' conditions. For example, depending on how we were feeling, we made tweaks to our environment such as moving to a comfortable armchair, writing with loud music playing (or turning it off all together), or writing outside in the sunshine.

It is not practically possible to create the perfect conditions for everyone in the classroom, but we can equip our students to think about how they might be better able to manage and adapt their classroom experience to boost their concentration, motivation and focus. The *move, manage and micro-manage* approach (Osborne et al., forthcoming 2023) helps both teachers *and* learners reflect on the importance of the environment in shaping our learning experience.

- *Move* enables the learner to consider what their optimum learning environment looks and feels like. For example, this might be a quiet space such as a library or a particular area of the classroom where they feel most comfortable and ready to learn.
- *Manage* enables the learner to consider adaptations that can be made (either by the teacher or student depending on what is possible): for example, considering the seating position in a classroom for neurodivergent learners in relation to sensory triggers such as light, noise, or other students squeezing past their seat.
- *Micro-manage* enables the learner to manage environmental stimuli at the micro level, which is particularly useful in a shared learning environment where learners may have different (and potentially conflicting) needs. This might include thinking about small but significant environmental factors such as the feel and shape of a particular pen, the type and colour of paper, or using mini- (non-distracting) movements such as drawing on a pad or moving their toes in their shoes to boost focus and concentration.

MANAGING OUR COMMUNICATION: COGNITIVE ACCESS TO SUBJECT KNOWLEDGE

One of the number one pressures which many teachers experience is having to get through a substantial amount of subject content in a limited amount of time. This pressure is particularly intense when preparing students for exams or in-class tests. Both the teacher and students can be left feeling like it is a race against time to get through the material!

Thinking about making our teaching content accessible and inclusive may at first seem like an additional challenge to manage. However, if we shift our focus slightly and consider *how* we convey our message, this can help to ensure that students take on board, process and retain teaching content effectively and more efficiently so that as much of our message as possible is successfully received at the first attempt. If we consider the example of a television advert, very little of the advert's key message gets lost as a lot of thought has gone into how to make the delivery of the content 'stick' and be remembered by the audience. While we can't always devote the same time and resource as a media marketing team, it can be a useful comparison to make.

Here are some strategies for busy teachers to help convey a message effectively to learners. We can use the strategies we outline here to ensure inclusive teaching delivery, as well as design effective resources, activities and assessments.

A PICTURE PAINTS A THOUSAND WORDS: DUAL CODING

Dual coding (Paivio, 1986) refers to the use of images, diagrams or infographs to support written or verbal descriptions. A well-chosen image can help to increase many students' capacity to process, retain and recall knowledge as we are not relying solely on one processing domain. The images we use do not have to be overly elaborate or complex. A simple image can help memory recall for some students and support a student's relational understanding as it can reinforce how the parts of a topic fit together or relate to one another. When using images, it is important to be mindful of the colours chosen as certain colours such as red and green might not be visible to students who have colour vision deficiency.

MOVING FROM CONCRETE TO ABSTRACT IDEAS OR MAKING LEARNING LINKS

Moving learners from prior to new learning can be vital to help students make connections and 'cement' new learning by linking it to what they already know. Simple and succinct summaries can help learners reinforce prior knowledge and provide vital context when new ideas are introduced. Remember that links to prior learning can be made across a lesson, week, term or year.

Providing examples can help students make meaningful connections between their everyday experience and new ideas which may be more abstract. Abstract thinking is only possible as the brain develops. Some adolescents (adolescence ranges from when puberty begins until the mid-20s) may have to wait longer than others before their prefrontal cortex sufficiently evolves, as we saw in **Chapter 4**. Remember that examples are most helpful when they are succinct (and do not cause the students to go off on a tangent). Metaphors may also help some students to move from the concrete to the abstract. Try to make sure the metaphors are universally understood so that the metaphors themselves do not become confusing and students can easily relate to the comparison you are making. This may be more problematic for students with DLD and ASC.

The simple phrase 'encounter, practise and master' (Jessop & Tomas, 2017) can help students to develop and consolidate their knowledge in a phased approach where they add detail and further context as they become more familiar with new concepts or ideas. Remember that some neurodivergent students may require longer in the practice phase before they can master some new knowledge or skill.

BIG PICTURE THINKING

When encountering a new idea for the first time, some of us are naturally drawn to details while others prefer to see the big picture first before making sense of the details. It can be helpful to use a simple cooking analogy to explore this idea further.

Some of us might start thinking about the overall type of meal we want to make. We may think about it in broad terms, by considering what type of dishes would go together or what type of flavours we want to create so the meal works as a whole.

Others might be more comfortable thinking about all the individual ingredients they require, the timings needed for each dish to be prepared and cooked. Knowing the details can boost confidence, provide reassurance and enable us to see the whole.

It is not that one way is right or better than the other but, as teachers, it is useful to think about both angles as a way into teaching a subject. When we have learnt or understand something, know our subject or have become an expert in our discipline, it is natural to start with the details (we may automatically have the big picture in mind). Educational textbooks often take this as their starting point. But for many students, particularly when they are being introduced to a topic for the first time, an overview is vital as it provides context. Access to an overall subject framework means that they can return to it again and again to reinforce and consolidate their learning as well. For example, this might involve making students explicitly aware to look for key universal themes when studying English literature, regardless of the passage or text they are reading. Similarly, showing how parts of a biology syllabus link together can help students make connections between the cellular, organ and body level, recognising the pattern that exists between structure and function.

BREAKING IT DOWN

Helping our students to break down information into manageable chunks can be very effective and boost students' ability to process, organise and recall new materials. Think about where your subject content lends itself to being broken down into chunks – but, when 'chunking' your content, remember to consider how the 'parts' fit together to form the whole.

Compare this approach with how to do a jigsaw (see Figure 8.2): it can be useful to think about how each of the pieces work together to contribute to the overall picture. As experts in our subjects, this can be hard to do as we may naturally and instinctively know how the individual pieces of the jigsaw work together. Try to spend some time thinking about the gaps rather than the pieces themselves; how could you help students move from one idea or concept to the next so they can see how a subject fits together?

It can be useful to take this analogy further and consider the different ways each of us might go about the task of completing a jigsaw: some might start with the edges first and use this to get a sense of the whole; others might focus on key parts of the picture and then fill in the gaps. Each of us will build our subject knowledge slightly differently and supporting learners to recognise this will help them to make links and 'complete' the puzzle of whatever they are learning at the time.

Figure 8.2   Jigsaw approach to seeing how a topic or subject fits together

MANAGING MICRO-METACOGNITION: FOSTERING EXPLORATION AND CURIOSITY ABOUT *HOW WE LEARN*

Metacognition is gaining traction as being central to learner success. This is of fundamental importance when supporting neurodivergent students to fulfil their potential. Metacognition essentially refers to when we *plan, monitor* and *evaluate*, and *make changes* to our own learning behaviours. As we can see in Figure 8.3, it is a continuous reflective cycle. It is about how we check and regulate the ways we think and learn. Metacognition is central to the inclusive classroom yet, to be impactful, we need to support learners to connect with it in a way that is tangible and meaningful to them.

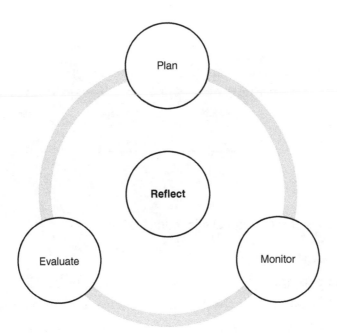

Figure 8.3   The cycle of metacognition

David Perkins (1992) says there are four levels of metacognitive learning, as shown in Figure 8.4. Here is a description of each level:

- *tacit*: we are unaware of our metacognitive knowledge. We don't think about any particular strategies for learning and merely accept if we know something or not;
- *aware*: we know about some of the kinds of thinking that we do, such as generating ideas, finding evidence, etc. However, our thinking is not necessarily deliberate or planned;
- *strategic*: we organise our thinking by using problem-solving, grouping and classifying, evidence-seeking and decision-making, etc. We know and apply the strategies that help us learn and progress;
- *reflective*: we are not only strategic about our thinking, but we also reflect upon our learning while it is happening, considering the success or not of any strategies we are using and then revising them as appropriate.

Figure 8.4   Levels of metacognitive learning

If we use the example of a recipe, someone who is *tacit* throws ingredients into a pot and hopes for the best; someone who is *aware* knows they could do better but are not sure what or how; someone who is *strategic* follows instructions and gets organised with the right equipment and measures; and someone who is *reflective* goes a step further, working out how to adapt and improve the recipe next time.

Note that reflection is not just an afterthought. As Donald Schön described in his work, we can reflect-*on*-action and reflect-*in*-action (Schön, 1987). By doing the latter it may take longer for us to complete a task, but it is likely that the end result will be better thought through. Note as well that, although the four levels of metacognitive learning are shown as a progressive arrow, all students will be at different levels depending on the task they are doing, and they may oscillate between them.

Micro-metacognition provides a useful tool (Osborne et al., forthcoming 2023) to enable students to reflect on and manage their own learning choices, and helps them move towards being reflective rather than tacit metacognitive learners. Instead of asking students to reflect on an activity or task as a whole, encourage them to consider it in a more nuanced way. Micro-metacognition fosters curiosity and exploration and provides a tangible means of 'thinking about thinking'.

Linking metacognition to cognitive comfort can provide a useful way of supporting this. For example, encourage learners to consider how they are affected by colour (pens, paper, etc.), space on a page (blank space versus lines, boxes, etc.), or how much a task is broken down. Micro-metacognition enables us to 'zoom in' on the nuts and bolts of how we learn and to make informed choices about how we interact with our environment to support effective cognition.

Micro-metacognition also involves building choice into a learning activity. For example, when engaging students in a planning exercise, instead of introducing just one tool such as a mind map or story board, introduce multiple means for students to capture their ideas on the page (e.g., a table, bullet points, separate pieces of paper, colour coding, using diagrams). As long as students reach the same destination, the routes there can be varied. We might call this differentiation by process.

Encourage students to take setbacks in their stride by moving from one strategy to another or combining them to overcome different hurdles. As their needs change and evolve, so too can the strategies they draw on. Remember to check in with students and remind or prompt them to move *between* strategies as they may not instinctively remember to navigate in a different direction. As learners become used to working in this way, they will require less prompting but it is important that students get used to new ways of working and build their confidence over a period of time.

MANAGING WELLBEING

As discussed in **Chapter 4**, there is a strong correlation between students with neurodivergent conditions and increased risks of having mental health challenges. Schools and teachers are increasingly being called upon to support learners' mental health as part of their overall educational provision. Yet, despite acknowledging the importance of student wellbeing, we tend to position this as something that exists beyond the classroom, as an antidote to the strains and pressures of learning.

While the rise of practices such as mindfulness, healthy eating, taking regular exercise and having good sleeping habits may be important for our mental health, wellbeing can also be better supported through the very ways in which we learn. We underestimate the link between *how* we think, learn and work and its impact on our wellbeing, and vice versa. The approaches to wellbeing we use in general may need to be adapted for those who are neurodivergent. Mindfulness approaches may need to be more 'mind-less' and incorporate movement as well, especially for a student who finds focusing harder to do.

The concept of 'welldoing' (Osborne et al., forthcoming 2023) is a way to consider the interconnected relationship between learning and wellbeing and provides a useful approach for the teacher so that we can better support learner wellbeing within the classroom via the everyday actions of teaching and learning (see Figure 8.5). For example, a child with neurodivergent traits who may be prone to analysis paralysis (see **Chapter 5**) and heightened anxiety may find it helpful to learn techniques which enable them to offset feelings associated with becoming overwhelmed, such as taking some exercise or using breathing techniques.

Wellbeing can also be directly supported via the process of teaching and learning itself. Clear and explicit teacher instructions and micro-metacognition techniques, such as using colour coding or tables for planning, enable the teacher and learner to manage wellbeing in a solution-focused, *anticipatory* way by removing, reducing or rethinking barriers. In this way we can both improve an individual's ability to learn and progress, and directly foster positive wellbeing.

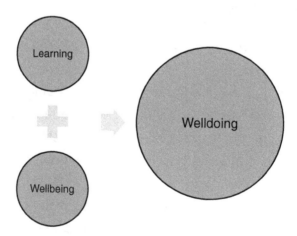

Figure 8.5   From wellbeing to welldoing

COACHING IN ORDER TO HELP STUDENTS TO GROW

You may want to use some facilitative coaching techniques with your students to help them reflect on the strategies they are using in their learning. One easy-to-remember mnemonic in coaching is GROW (Whitmore, 2017):

G   your **goal**

R   the **reality** of where you are now in your approach to learning

O   the **options** you have for alternative strategies

W   what you **will do** next and your commitment to it.

Many students find it difficult to know where to start when being asked to reflect, but the GROW technique can help them divide what looks like a daunting task into chunks. They can then consider, with the support of their teacher, where they are now and what they might need for the next step.

The options stage may require some trial and error, perhaps watching how others do the same task and mimicking or adapting what they do. You may want to use a template to help students record each of the stages and steps, and particularly the final commitment for action.

A key part of coaching is for the learner to think for themselves. This involves the use of open questions and the teacher holding back on giving an opinion. Open questions all either begin with or contain the letters W and H, for example:

- What could you do differently next time?
- Which resources would you need?
- Who in the class is doing the task in a way that you would like to try?
- When in your approach to the task do you think you should do this?
- How would you feel if you did this step before that step?

Coaching exists on a continuum that starts (at the mentoring end) with telling someone what to do, depending on the degree of 'push' or 'pull' that is needed, as shown in Figure 8.6, starting top left and following the arrows.

All students – whether or not they are neurodivergent – can benefit from appropriate coaching-style interventions facilitated by their teacher according to where they are in their learning cycle.

Figure 8.6   The coaching continuum (adapted from Downey, 2014)

For coaching and self-regulative techniques to work well, the teacher and student need to be ready. This involves creating a positive, caring environment, where students feel the teacher will listen to them actively and without prejudice. Listening actively is a hard skill for any of us to learn, as we may be tempted to jump in and give the answer or advice if we know it. A more powerful way of helping students to help themselves is to give *them* the time and the space to do so. They may make sudden great leaps, or they may make a series of cumulative marginal gains (see **Chapter 7**).

As educators, we need to set a good example that our students can learn from, which includes being patient and cognisant about how our students may go through a range of feelings as they learn how to function more productively. Being approachable, available and having the right attitude will give neurodivergent learners greater confidence to learn how to learn for themselves.

A TRANSFERABLE APPROACH WITHIN
AND BEYOND THE CLASSROOM

In the previous chapter we discussed how effective strategies, once identified and embedded in one area of our practice, can be transferred and applied to other areas of our teaching (see Figure 7.7, page 97). If you have found a strategy works well in your teaching, the chances are it will also work equally well when applied to the resources and assessments you use.

Just as we can 'transfer' the inclusive approaches we develop to different aspects of teaching practice, our students can also transfer the same approaches beyond the classroom. For example, if the student finds an approach like micro-metacognition is effective in the classroom, they may also like to consider how the same approach could be applied in other learning contexts in the wider school setting, such as physical activities. Could the approach be used for other subjects by teaching colleagues? Could the approach also be used in the wider school community to support inclusive pastoral care? As we have mentioned throughout this book, effective strategies are rarely limited to one setting or context.

Furthermore, there is real value in thinking outside the box and considering how an effective approach could be adapted and used by a student beyond the class or school environment. The key to achieving this lies in our ability to *adapt* the approach depending on the context, task and individual's need, or it can be easy to fall into the habit of associating a specific strategy or intervention with one specific context or subject area.

A transferable approach to inclusivity not only enables the individual to make the most of the strategies that are available to them but also helps to cement effective habits and behaviours. If a student uses a strategy in only one context, there is limited opportunity to revisit the strategy, to consolidate the approach and use it in a way that is habit forming. Supporting students to see the transferability of strategies they use will not only help them to grow in confidence but also to recognise how important such skills are. An effective skill honed in the classroom, such as using colour coding to organise information, is not only a learning skill but will also help in employment and managing daily life.

Finally, but importantly, we can sometimes fall into the habit of associating one strategy with a particular student in a specific context. However, while a student may have a tried and tested strategy in one context, it may not always work every time or in every situation. By encouraging students to explore a range of approaches, we better equip them with the confidence and ability to move *between* strategies. As we have already mentioned, remember to introduce strategies gradually in a way that the learners are comfortable with. Inclusive education is just as much a process which takes time and refinement for the students as it is for the teachers.

If we draw (again) on an analogy from cooking, we might have our go-to recipe, technique or tool for cooking our own favourite, tried and tested dishes, but (although there are some key rules to follow!) there are countless methods which can be adapted, modified and combined. Think of how many recipes there are for making bread around the world: although the techniques, tools and methods may vary, the recipes will all lead to tasty bread! When we apply this thinking in the classroom (and beyond), it moves us away from an ideal which all learners should adhere to and instead helps to build in choice and foster creativity and autonomy.

Support students to pick and mix strategies, combine and adapt them depending on their needs at that time and the context in which they find themselves. Take small steps to develop your inclusive teaching practice over time, and work with your students and colleagues to explore creative solutions to help them overcome barriers both within the classroom and beyond.

KEY TAKEAWAYS

- Inclusive education is a shared space between teachers, and learners.
- As teachers and students, we can manage our environment to boost concentration, focus and motivation.

- As teachers we can employ a range of techniques to ensure students can fully access and make use of the knowledge we present to them.
- Metacognition is fundamental to the inclusive classroom and works best when we support students to explore their own metacognition at a more nuanced level (micro-metacognition).
- We can support wellbeing via the very ways in which we teach and our students learn.
- Coaching techniques provide a powerful approach for the teacher to help students develop and grow.
- Once we have identified effective and impactful inclusive strategies, we can transfer and embed this *across* our teaching practice, and beyond the classroom.

9

ASSESSING NEURODIVERSE LEARNERS

In this chapter we will consider:

- the basic principles and practices of educational assessment;
- the barriers some students will encounter in showing what they know and can do;
- how we can reduce and remove barriers to assessment for neurodivergent learners;
- what we could do to make summative assessments more inclusive;
- what we could do to support students in their preparation for summative assessments, including our approach to formative assessments.

THE ASSESSMENT OF KNOWLEDGE, SKILLS AND UNDERSTANDING

The assessment of knowledge, skills and understanding is something that is integral to life at and beyond school. It has many purposes and many uses, often holding the key to the door to what we are permitted to do next. The influence of assessment on what and how students learn is so strong that the term 'backwash effect' is sometimes used to show its impact on the curriculum and pedagogy. This effect may be positive or negative, resulting in strategies that advance students' approaches to learning, or those that encourage more superficial approaches, such as 'teaching to the test'.

The influence of grades generated from summative assessments also has an impact on how a school's performance – or the success of a government's educational policies – are perceived. This may, in turn, lead to some students, who it is presumed will reduce a school's average, being denied the opportunity to take certain exams. Or it may lead to attempts to 'play' the system by giving by some means an unfair advantage to those students who don't merit it. Both of these consequences can be to the disadvantage of neurodivergent students.

There is a large body of research behind assessment, and it has become a big industry. Lots of people working in education have a good grounding in the principles and practices of assessment but the level of confidence becomes weaker – even among the biggest experts – the more we venture into questions around the *accessibility* of traditional forms of assessment, and their impact on the wellbeing of students. There is much still to be done to shape the future of educational assessments so that they become less daunting and more inclusive. As we shall see, there are lessons that can be applied from the principles of universal design, which underline the importance of considering teaching, learning and assessment concurrently rather than in isolation from each other.

While thinking about how we could improve summative assessments, it is important to bear in mind that any changes in practices would take time. This is not only because of the body of evidence that has been produced to support the status quo and the extent of the commercial opportunities in educational assessment as it currently exists and operates, but also because it is not a quick task to convince all stakeholders – including the general population – that new ways are as good as or better than the old. You may remember our references to 'the average person' and 'standardisation' earlier in this book. It is hard – but not impossible – to break habits about how we measure ourselves against others.

We can, nevertheless, strive as teachers to change how we assess students *formatively* so that we do so by preparing more inclusively. We already explored in **Chapter 8** how we can facilitate students' thinking about using a variety of ways to approach a task. Later in this chapter we will consider what else we could do to support all students to be better prepared for summative assessments in their current form.

THE BASIC PRINCIPLES AND PRACTICES OF EDUCATIONAL ASSESSMENT

Educational assessment can be defined as: 'the process of gathering and recording evidence about a learner's response to a planned task' (Child & Ellis, 2021, p. 8). We explain below what we mean by 'task' – you'll soon see that there's a lot of jargon in the assessment world! Assessment is the means by which we can discover whether students have learnt what they have been taught so that we can reflect on and plan our teaching for the subsequent steps in their learning; or so that decisions can be made about or by an individual, with others' support and expertise, as to their readiness and suitability for the next proposed stage in their life, such as continuing education or a starting a job.

Assessment can be formative or summative, depending on how the evidence is employed. It may be used to help us see where a learner is now in relation to where they are intending to go and what they need to do to get there – we call this assessment *for* learning. Or it may be used at the end of a period of learning to make a judgement about the standard someone has achieved. This is known as assessment *of* learning.

From an educator's perspective, both types of assessment essentially involve three steps, deciding:

1. what you want to know more about;
2. how you are going to gather and record the evidence; and
3. how you are going to process the evidence.

CONSTRUCTS

What you want to know more about is called a 'construct'. A construct is a proposed attribute of a person that may be *directly* measurable – for example, their height, or *indirectly* measurable – for example, their mathematical ability.

Your means of gathering and recording evidence in relation to the construct could be various, such as through practical tasks, writing under exam conditions, or coursework. The way that you process the evidence will, first, be to evaluate it using a measurement tool and then to decide what to do with the data. Table 9.1 gives you three examples of how you could collect and interpret evidence at and beyond school.

Table 9.1 Collecting and interpreting evidence

Assessment	Evidence	Measurement tool or standard	Evaluation
A level exam	Completed script	Mark scheme	Examiner marks using mark scheme
Driving test	Driving a car and completing manoeuvres	Driving test report form	Driving examiner notes faults
Observation while operating a machine	Completing a task using a specific machine	Operating checklist (instructions or guidelines)	Assessor uses the operating checklist to evaluate the applicant's capability to use the machine safely

VALIDITY

Regardless of the end use of an assessment, it needs to have *validity* if it is going to meet its stated purpose. At its most basic, validity is a means of judging whether an assessment measures what it claims to measure. But it is also about the conclusions made from the evaluation of the assessment and what is done with these conclusions.

To be more precise, it is *construct validity* that is considered the key aspect of assessment. Construct validity can be defined as:

> The degree to which the assessment that you have created assesses the abilities which are the focus of the course or curriculum. Construct validity therefore relies on a sound description of the construct that you are interested in and a clear understanding of how it is being measured.
>
> (Child & Ellis, 2021, p. 17)

To use again a word that we have frequently seen throughout this book, we can easily imagine that several aspects of an assessment may *interfere* with its potential to be valid. In assessment terminology, these interferences are known as 'threats', and there are two main ones:

1. when some elements of the knowledge, skills and understanding we would like to measure are missing (known as *construct under-representation*); and

2. when the performance of an individual who is taking an assessment is impacted in a way that is not relevant to their ability in relation to what we are measuring (known as *construct-irrelevant variance*).

If we take a couple of examples from Table 9.1 to illustrate each of the two threats:

1. a student may have learnt topics that were on the syllabus but have been inadvertently omitted from the examination they are taking;
2. an apprentice may be observed operating a machine that hasn't been serviced properly and so doesn't work in the way they might normally expect.

The second of the two threats is clearly important when we are considering neurodivergent learners who may find traditional forms and means of assessment unsuitable to their needs and the ways in which they function. We shall explore this in more detail below. Until relatively recently, little thought was given to the barriers that prevent some students showing what they know in either summative or formative assessments. Many were excluded from assessments or simply got poor grades.

RELIABILITY

The validity of an assessment also depends on its *reliability*, which is about how consistently it would measure and give the same result in two identical sets of circumstances from when an assessment is designed until the evidence it produces is graded. Inevitably, a lot of assessment that takes place is unreliable, a major source of which is human bias and error, which may or may not be unconscious.

The relative importance of reliability in assessment will depend on the nature and purpose of an assessment, as well as its manageability. It is unrealistic for the same conditions to be replicated each time an assessment is taken and for a busy teacher to ensure that any type of test – be it small or large – conforms to the strict definition of reliability. Assessment organisations use a lot of data and research to track reliability in summative assessments across a whole cohort of students, but teachers seldom repeat exactly the same in-class, formative assessment, so it could be argued that test reliability is less important for them.

FAIRNESS

The last assessment principle for us to consider is *fairness*. This can be with regard to processes and procedures and also bias and accessibility before, during and after an assessment. Again, assessment organisations these days take this into account in the design of exams, often using checklists or an 'accessibility review' matrix. You may have spotted that fairness in assessment is a close cousin of construct-irrelevant variance.

When investigating the validity of an assessment, you need to consider the extent to which *all* students who are taking it have an equitable opportunity to demonstrate their ability. There is a danger otherwise that we are once again just comparing all students to what the fictitious 'average' student is expected to do – and that those who are neurodivergent may be at a disadvantage.

Assessment organisations do a lot of the heavy lifting when it comes to high-stakes summative assessments, such as GCSEs and A Levels. They work hard at validity, reliability and fairness for all students who will be tested, and provide strict guidelines about how, where and under what conditions an assessment should be taken, including with regard to so-called 'access arrangements', as we shall see below. Even though a teacher can't be expected to replicate this every day, because we don't have the wherewithal or capacity to do so, we should still do our best to make our in-class formative and summative assessments as inclusive as we can. If you lack confidence in doing so, start small and gradually build up what you know and can do.

REDUCING AND REMOVING INTERFERENCES IN AN ASSESSMENT

ENVIRONMENT

We have already seen in previous chapters how your environment can have a positive or negative impact on how you feel and function. Imagine now a typical exam room, with rows of desks separated at a precise distance, maybe floors and walls that echo to the scrape of chair legs or the scratching of pens, harsh lighting, uncomfortable temperature ... You would struggle to find someone who would feel completely at ease in this setting.

If then you are someone who finds it hard to sit still on a hard chair for any length of time, or finds the sounds made by other people distracting, or bright lights difficult to endure, you will already be at a disadvantage. The student who needs more time to respond or has difficulties with hand-writing is disadvantaged too. The student with spelling or reading challenges will find a fixed-time response harder as well. Would some of these students placed in a quiet room or provided with a computer or an open-book exam showcase their abilities more effectively? Think back to what we discussed in **Chapter 7** with regard to helping students remove interferences in their teaching and learning, from a *physical*, *cognitive* and *cultural* perspective. The same principles should ideally apply in assessment.

ACCESS ARRANGEMENTS

Regulators have designed strict rules that assessment organisations need to adhere to in their guidance to schools about exam conditions, and what can be done for students who need support. Such support, requested pre-examination, is commonly termed as 'access arrangements' and is designed to allow learners who qualify – through an identified condition or injury – to access an assessment without changing the demands of that assessment. A wide array of access arrangements is available, ranging from larger font sizes on exam papers to being assisted by an adult in writing, reading or by prompting, and sometimes taking the assessment in a separate room away from other distractions. The aim of access arrangements is to remove construct-irrelevant variance.

Something that some schools neglect is the need for students who will have access arrangements to practise them – and also to be allowed them as far as is manageable in classroom tests or mock examinations. Carmen Vidal Rodeiro (2021), who has undertaken a lot of research into access arrange-ments, writes that:

The principle of the access arrangement to align with the student's normal way of working aims to ensure that students are not introduced to an unknown procedure or technology during the assessment; familiarity is an important consideration if the arrangement is to be beneficial for the candidate.

(p. 9)

One very common access arrangement that has regularly been shown to make assessment more equitable is additional time – usually 25 per cent. If you have two three-hour exams in the same day, this can add up to an extra 90 minutes – or a total of 7.5 hours – in the exam room, which is a lot for anyone (including invigilators)! There appears to be no evidence-based reason why 25 per cent is the figure that is conventionally used, but that it is more to do with making additional time easier to administer.

Vidal Rodeiro's (2021) and others' research suggests that additional time may offer some high-school students an unfair advantage as they are given more time than is reasonable for their specific needs to read questions and write their responses. Studies by Helen Duncan and Catherine Purcell (2017, 2019) suggest university-level students do not gain an advantage. If students are given additional time, many studies point to the need for them to gain appropriate skills in the use of this time, as we will mention again in the final section of this chapter. It is also of greater benefit for many students if they can use a word processor, with or without additional time.

Some studies indicate that students may be more likely than others to gain access arrangements depending on the school they attend or their parents' ability to pay for diagnosis. There is a suggestion too, as Rodeiro says, that 'students' characteristics [such as their ethnicity] may influence teachers' decisions about which students need access arrangements' (2021, p. 10). Owing to the large volume of entries made for examinations, assessment organisations have to trust schools to do what is right for their students, while acknowledging it is not always a scientific process or free from bias.

As teachers, we should also design and administer our *formative* assessments with accessibility in mind, taking note of the arrangements available for summative assessments. For example, do some students need:

- use of a digital device to write their answers in a vocabulary test?
- support in carrying or handling scientific equipment when performing an experiment?
- a less distracting environment or a window to look out of when writing an essay?
- larger print for a reading comprehension?
- music scores for sight reading on non-white paper or an adjustable digital screen?

This may sound like substantial extra work – and there is no denying that it may be initially. But, as we similarly described in previous chapters, the more we get used to designing assessments from the outset with inclusivity in mind and embrace the concept of neurodiversity, the more we should not only appreciate the need to make all forms of assessment as valid and fair for all as we can but also become adept at doing so.

TEST ANXIETY

Apart from the relative discomfort of the exam room or assessment demands, test stress can play a large role in students' success. Stress can be turned into something positive for some students as they find it motivating and it activates hormones that give them a boost. For many, though, stress translates into anxiety (see **Chapter 4**), which tends to be higher in neurodivergent students (unless they are hyper-focused), leading them to do less well in educational assessments.

Test anxiety is normally due to:

- an individual's self-beliefs;
- their interactions with others; or
- the nature of an assessment (such as whether it is an oral exam, a science practical or a paper requiring answers to be written in essay form); and
- an individual's lack of effective strategies to manage stressful situations.

We already discussed in **Chapter 4** how a student's perception of their own ability and their motivation can have an impact on how they feel and function.

The psychologist Albert Ellis, working in the 1950s, devised a technique that was subsequently developed by Martin Seligman to help people 'talk' themselves through anxiety-provoking events.

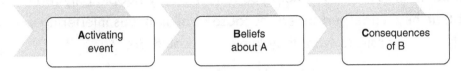

Figure 9.1   The ABC model of anxiety management (acknowledgement: David Putwain, 2021)

If we use the thought process illustrated in Figure 9.1, we can consider how a student might feel about a forthcoming exam (A). If, on the one hand, they believe they are going to do badly, their emotional response (B) may be that they become anxious and their behavioural response (C) that they withdraw effort. If, on the other hand, they believe they could do well (B), they will be more hopeful and prepare the best they can for the exam (C).

In a similar way to what was described with regard to levels of metacognition in **Chapter 8**, we would need to support some students in their understanding of such a model, so that they know they may have different beliefs about different assessment situations and that the consequences will not always be the same. It may, however, help those who are more likely to be anxious to know *why* and *how* their response can make a difference to how successful they are.

A major factor in some students' anxiety around tests can be the influence of others. They may compare themselves favourably or unfavourably to their peers or they may be positively or negatively affected by the pressure put on them by their parents or teachers. As we have discussed already, our neurodiverse world by definition means we should not impose our expectations on others, as we are individuals on our own pathways and will react in our own ways according to context. Often well-meaning suggestions made by adults about the consequences of not studying hard or getting high grades demonstrate *their* beliefs or fears rather than those of the young person.

It is interesting to look back as an adult and consider the extent to which your own ability to 'show what you know' was negatively impacted by factors not under your control or of which you were unaware. Table 9.2 uses Gallwey's formula from our **Introduction** to summarise what we have covered in this section and help you reflect. Many people only realise much later that they 'underperformed' because of all that was interfering with their ability to demonstrate what they knew and could do.

Table 9.2   Gallwey's formula and interference in educational assessments

Performance	Potential	Interference
Assessment score or grade	What a learner knows or can do relative to a specific subject and level of study (with additional support, such as through access arrangements)	• environment • other people • self (anxiety) • content of exam paper • nature of exam questions • type of information or recording style required

RETHINKING ASSESSMENTS FOR NEURODIVERGENT LEARNERS

What could be done in the creation of assessments to make them less daunting and more inclusive in our neurodiverse world? In **Chapter 5** we explored universal design for learning. Researchers have built on this to propose the universal design of assessments (UDA). The US National Center on Educational Outcomes (n.d.) describes the elements of UDA to improve assessment validity and accessibility, that would include:

- precisely defined constructs;
- non-biased items (assessment tasks and mark schemes);
- simple, clear and intuitive instructions and procedures;
- maximum readability and comprehensibility;
- maximum legibility.

Many respected assessment organisations already follow similar guidelines and have developed their own accessibility review checklists to be used for every element of an examination – from the language used in questions and multiple-choice answers, to images, to what font is chosen. It is not always the case, however, that inclusivity is a primary consideration when the design of a brand-new summative assessment begins.

THE 3 As OF ASSESSMENT

Child and Ellis (2021) suggest some ways of making assessments more appropriate and authentic, as well as accessible – what they call the '3 As'. Others have proposed another 'A' – 'automated', although it could be argued that this is more a tool than a principle, and has the potential to support assessments in becoming more appropriate and authentic.

The *appropriacy* of an assessment returns us to its intended purpose and what is done with the resulting evidence. A greater understanding now by educators of data – and the invention of more sophisticated software to manage the data – could enable teachers to make better and more immediate decisions about what to do next in supporting an individual student's learning pathway or readiness to move onto the next step.

Appropriacy can also be about what is manageable, which may help with decisions regarding the validity or reliability of an assessment, resulting in greater fairness for all. Assessments can be automated so that the questions asked of students are more appropriate to them according to their responses to previous questions. This is known as computerised adaptive testing.

The *authenticity* of an assessment is about its applicability to – or place in – the real world. Many students see exam questions as abstract and may perform better if the questions were placed in an authentic context rather than on an exam paper in a distracting exam hall – this is particularly the case for some neurodivergent individuals who see more literal meaning in what they read or hear. The vocational education sector is much better at authenticity than more academic settings, and perhaps the latter could learn something about the benefits of establishing a meaningful context to demonstrate what a student knows and can do.

Again, automated or digital devices can assist in making assessments more authentic. A student might be assessed in real time and in situ when they are ready rather than having to go to another, unfamiliar room at another time. Another student could record their progress in a portfolio-style assessment to demonstrate the process of their learning rather than just the end result. And, to return to something more fundamental, it may soon be time to stop requiring students to write by hand in exams, as it is more authentic and normal nowadays for the majority of us to use a computer keyboard.

By making some assessments more appropriate and authentic in some of the ways described and others, we could quickly make them more valid, accessible, inclusive and, hopefully, less likely to provoke anxiety. With the combined effort of researchers, teachers, parents and young people – and by ensuring we listen to the voices of those who find the ways in which we currently test and grade in education challenging – we could make assessments much more equitable for all learners.

SUPPORTING ALL LEARNERS TO PREPARE FOR ASSESSMENTS

While summative assessments remain in their current form, there is plenty teachers could do to support learners in their preparations. We can use similar approaches in our formative assessments in class, and start from a young age so that students have learnt good habits and techniques by the time assessments get more serious towards the end of their schooling.

AWARENESS AND UNDERSTANDING

We should start by making sure we are aware of each individual student's needs and in encouraging all students to understand and be considerate of the needs of each other. We can do this through raising awareness and having open discussions about why some students require more help than others in certain situations, such as the taking of assessments. We should apply for and confirm any access arrangements in good time, so that learners – and those supporting them – have time to practise and familiarise themselves with the regulations and parameters.

REVISION AND EXAM TECHNIQUES

As we suggested in **Chapter 8**, we may need to help some students to gain skills to understand how to be organised. This will particularly be the case when they need to revise for an assessment. Organisational skills may include learning how to break down a large amount of material, highlighting what is important, or designing a revision timetable – we need to take care, though, that some students don't get too obsessed by the colours they are using or fretting when things don't go to plan. Consider how micro-metacognition techniques could help your students put in place organisational strategies which are adaptable and reflect their changing needs.

For the assessment itself, it is a good idea to 'walk' students through a specimen paper, so they can see and even touch it. Familiarise students with the ways in which questions are worded, so that they understand the meaning of the 'command' words telling them what to do – a glossary of exam terms and phrases, such as 'explain', 'compare', 'contrast', can be very helpful. Give them practice in reading and rereading questions, and in common errors that can be picked up through proofreading. Help them understand as well that they can often do an exam in any order they want, and how to manage this in a timed situation.

To get ready for the exam day, some students will benefit from visiting the location of the assessment, and maybe even rehearsing the whole journey from home to there. It can be a good idea as well to work with students to devise checklists for what equipment to take with them, including something to drink or eat, according to what is permitted.

And, although we spoke at the beginning of this chapter about the extent to which assessment is integral to all our lives, we may also want to encourage students to engage in cognitive behavioural therapy techniques, such as mindfulness, so that they can put their successes or otherwise into perspective. We all know of friends, family and famous people who have gone on to enjoy positive lives and careers despite their exam grades. We want to give all students maximum opportunity to do well in their assessments – through current or future methods of making tests as valid, reliable, fair and accessible as possible – but there are countless other ways of showing and knowing what we can do.

KEY TAKEAWAYS

- Educational assessments are based on a long-established set of principles and practices that have been adjusted over time so that more students are able to demonstrate their knowledge, skills and understanding.
- Tests can be stressful situations for many students, but particularly for those who are neurodivergent and having to deal with multiple barriers to perform to their potential.
- Some assessments could be better designed so that students do not need to apply for special access arrangements, so that they cause less anxiety, or so that they are less abstract in nature.
- Digital technology – and sharing modes of assessment across educational settings – should open up new possibilities for making educational assessment fairer and more inclusive.
- There are many ways in which we can support all students – whether or not they are neurodivergent – to prepare for and perform better in assessments.

10

NEURODIVERSITY IN THE EDUCATION WORKPLACE

In this chapter we will consider:

- what it is like to be a neurodivergent teacher;
- how we can improve our education workplaces so that they recognise neuro-diverse needs and differences;
- how the concepts we have discussed in this book are applicable to adults as well as to young people;
- how to work with parents of learners who are neurodivergent;
- what we can do to continue to develop ourselves as education professionals.

NOT ALL TEACHERS ARE THE SAME

If it is estimated that around 15 per cent – or one in six – people are neuro-divergent, there must be many teachers who process information differently to what is considered typical. Throughout this book we have spoken about the need to recognise – and celebrate – neurodiversity in young people, and in the same vein we should do so in adults working in education (and else-where). We need to consider what adjustments or adaptations neurodivergent teachers require so that they can feel and function as well as possible in their roles. Additionally, we need to welcome and attract them to the education profession by ensuring our recruitment and retention policies and procedures are inclusive. Indeed, we may consider that the experiences and insights of a neurodivergent teacher would be advantageous in every school.

Until recently, many teachers have hidden that they are neurodivergent – or they may only have discovered this later in life, perhaps when one of their students (or one of their children) has been diagnosed with one or more conditions. Some people who are neurodivergent will never have made it into a role in education, even though they would have made excellent teachers. Either anxiety, imposter syndrome, the recruitment and training processes, or the perceived demands of the role may have dissuaded or discouraged them.

Many neurodivergent teachers who have successfully survived in the education system so far continually fear being found out and judged as 'surplus to requirements' if their managers consider they have weaknesses rather than see their strengths. They may be worried that others would consider their neurodivergence as a threat to the high standards their workplace purports to uphold, whereas we would, of course, subscribe to the view that our collective but varied neurodiversity in the teaching profession makes education much richer and more impactful for students.

WHAT IS IT LIKE TO BE A NEURODIVERGENT TEACHER?

All of us usually find something challenging in our professional lives but, once again, is this because of who we are or as a result of the environment and the people with whom we interact? What is interfering with us performing to our potential in the education profession? We probably all know fellow teachers, including ourselves, who will have struggled with certain aspects of the job. Some may find it hard to plan lessons or remember to bring the right resources; others will need extra time to mark work or write reports; still others may have a reputation for bad handwriting or a messy room. Not all these teachers would reach the diagnostic threshold for a neurodivergent condition, but some may do if they were formally assessed.

There is relatively little research into the experiences of teachers who have been diagnosed with neurodivergent traits, although Lisa Jacobs, Jonathan Glazzard and other colleagues (2021) have documented and highlighted in their academic work the experiences of teachers with dyslexia (about 10 per cent of the UK population has dyslexia). Some recently published books, including one edited by Rebecca Wood et al. (2022), are starting to present ideas and experiences about what it is like for some neurodivergent individuals joining or working in the teaching profession.

On the *positive* side, anecdotal evidence suggests that:

- neurodivergence (or disability, as quoted in one study) can be seen by some teachers as an asset and a reason to get into teaching, to present a role model for neurodivergent students and give them a better experience than the neurodivergent (or disabled) teachers themselves had at school;
- some schools deliberately seek to employ neurodivergent teachers because they consider them more caring, empathetic, passionate, creative, able to see patterns and explain topics in novel ways, and therefore particularly adept at working with young people – especially where there are barriers to learning;
- if a neurodivergent teacher has a good mentor early in their career, it can help with confidence and support ways of overcoming or learning to cope with challenges and building on strengths;
- some neurodivergent teachers' special interests can enthuse students and encourage this passion for learning with their students.

On the *negative* side, research so far suggests that:

- neurodivergent teachers may have lower self-esteem resulting from poor previous experiences in education or from a reinforcement of a focus on their weaknesses rather than their strengths;
- there are increasing demands in the curriculum across all subjects for students – and therefore teachers often need to be able to use all four communicative skills (listening, reading, writing, speaking). Many neurodivergent teachers will have a range of strategies of their own that they can share with students but the extra expectations regarding language use in teaching and learning may lead to additional pressure and strain;
- some neurodivergent teachers, without the use of scaffolding tools, may at times take longer to prepare lessons, give written feedback on student work, or respond to parents' emails. However, we should not stereotype and presume all neurodivergent teachers will have the same needs or require the same types of support.

By taking many of the same principles for students we can also help support many neurodivergent teachers. Think back, for example to **Chapter 7**, where we talked about 'patterns beyond labels'. How could our education environments and working practices be updated to consider all teachers' physical, cultural and cognitive needs, rather than just assuming that one size fits all?

RECRUITING AND ONBOARDING NEURODIVERGENT STAFF

If we value cognitive differences and want to attract teachers who are neurodivergent, we need to reflect on our approaches to recruitment and onboarding. In Table 10.1 we have written a ten-point checklist to help your education workplace to be more neuro-inclusive.

Table 10.1   Neurodiverse recruitment checklist

		Yes/no/ could do better
1	In the advertisement we have used inclusive and welcoming language, stating clearly who we are and specifically what role we are seeking to fill.	
2	In the job description, rather than using a phrase such as 'would need to have good interpersonal skills', we have said 'the candidate must be able to demonstrate an ability to communicate and work well with others to meet deadlines'. We have avoided listing 'desirable skills'.	
3	If we are asking for a covering letter or CV, we have stated how many pages or words are required, and we haven't asked for the same information to be repeated on a template application form.	
4	In the application procedure we have warmly encouraged candidates to disclose/share whether they need adjustments or access arrangements, and we have ensured that our sifting and interview process would not unfairly discriminate against such candidates.	
5	If the application procedure is online, we have checked and can state that we adhere to local legislation regarding digital accessibility.	
6	If the role for which someone is applying does not require IT skills (such as an invigilator or lunchtime supervisor) but the application process is normally online, we are offering an alternative route so that it is more inclusive and doesn't test skills we are not asking for.	

	Yes/no/ could do better
7 When a candidate is invited for interview, we are explicit about the expectations, location and who will be on the panel. We offer adjustments at this point again in the process.	
8 When we interview, we have a clear protocol of questions that we have tested so that what we are asking is relevant to the post, clear and fair for all candidates, and we also include sufficient flexibility for a candidate to demonstrate what they know and can do. Before the interview we indicate the nature of questions we will ask.	
9 At the end of the interview, we state when we will let the candidate know whether they have been successful and we ensure that we do as we say.	
10 When we have decided who is the successful candidate, we have a procedure for giving appropriate, constructive feedback in a timely manner to all candidates.	

STARTING IN THE JOB

When beginning in a job it is important that a new colleague knows what is expected of them in the role. This starts from when they are offered a position, in preparation for when it begins, and in the initial weeks, months or even year of starting. To be as inclusive as possible, think about the format in which the information is given – for example, could long documents be presented in a more user-friendly manner, with an executive summary or optionally in other formats such as audio, a video, or self-study presentation slides? The suggestions made in previous chapters about communication for young people are also applicable for adults, going beyond thinking about adjustments in terms of purely in physical terms – for example, a change in font style or the use of coloured paper.

Getting support in place in a timely manner can make a big difference to someone feeling engaged in a new job and being their most productive. When you have a new starter – whether they are neurodivergent or not – it can be helpful to set up regular short meetings to check how things are going. This can mean that feedback is provided promptly and, if required, any small adaptations can be put in place. It can be harder for some people to know if they are doing okay if they have no opportunity to discuss their progress or compare it against previous benchmarks. Some people may be reticent to ask for guidance as they may have had poor past experiences and lack confidence in doing so. Having a work buddy or mentor can help soften initial anxieties and help a new teacher navigate what is often a complex working environment.

HELPING NEURODIVERGENT TEACHERS REACH THEIR POTENTIAL

In schools and other education workplaces, there are at least five common areas where we could reconsider our typical practices to make them more inclusive.

THE CLASSROOM

Sometimes a teacher will have a room that is assigned to them and where they do most or all their teaching. Often, a new recruit will, however, be required to move from room to room. This may result from a school's policy that no teacher has a dedicated classroom, but it may also be because certain members of staff are rewarded with their own space for no other reason than their long service or hierarchical status. It may be wiser instead to consider where individual teachers work best – while not forgetting as well that this applies to both new and more experienced teachers, who may also have neurodivergent requirements, which may or may not be documented.

A teacher's working environment can make a considerable difference to how they perform. A teacher may be affected by the temperature, sound, light and smells – staff who look after the facilities should be encouraged to act as soon as possible on requests for heating to be adjusted, soundproofing to be improved or flickering bulbs to be changed. Teachers are not deliberately trying to create extra work when they make requests – it is usually for the benefit of teaching and learning.

Some individuals need to have an organised workplace and would be upset if other teachers were to disrupt their materials or desk layout. At a staff meeting, you may want to discuss and agree on the state in which a shared classroom should be left at the end of every lesson – for example, should all chairs be tucked under tables, and should the whiteboard be wiped clean? Having a tidy environment can make a positive difference to the start of a lesson and play to the strengths of a neurodivergent teacher (or student) who prefers everything to be in what for them is the 'right' place. Regular dialogue between teachers working in shared spaces can avoid conflict.

THE STAFFROOM

Staffrooms are shared spaces, and it is part of being a colleague to adapt to this environment. Sometimes teachers have their own desk, cupboard and mug. Are the rules clear in your staffroom? Again, are certain members of staff given unwarranted advantages over other members of staff who may otherwise feel more comfortable? Understanding that some people find it hard to share their cups, plates, etc., or have sensitivities to certain food odours, can reduce the risk of issues occurring.

Whether in a shared space such as a staffroom or elsewhere in the education workplace, is there a space that teachers can go to sit quietly or work without distraction? Are there rooms for private conversations? Is there somewhere that staff can genuinely take a break without being disturbed by students or other teachers?

STAFF MEETINGS

As we have learnt throughout this book, our neurodiverse world contains people who act and respond in multiple ways. Some are more outgoing than others, whereas others find being in a group challenging. An expert leader – be they the principal or another member of staff – should learn how to get the best out of all their staff, so that all opinions are heard and listened to without prejudice.

Staff meetings can be intimidating experiences, especially for new recruits and for some who are neurodivergent. There may be many individuals who are too self-conscious to contribute to an open discussion but who have something pertinent to say that they could express in advance, by proxy or anonymously. If we want to encourage a neurodiverse workforce, we need to provide opportunities for everyone to give input in a manner of their choosing, and not force people into uncomfortable situations. For some teachers, attending meetings online rather than in person may allow them to be more involved.

Many meetings – in education or other workplaces – are poorly run. To get the most out of a meeting, regardless of who is attending, we need to think of its purpose, why we have invited certain people to attend and what we hope to achieve. The reasons for and objectives of a meeting, as well as the agenda and any documents to read, should be shared in advance to give all participants enough time to prepare. We should minute the key points and actions and share them in a timely manner. Being clear about how people can engage and ensuring a means to do so will also be important especially if some teachers need a little longer to think, process and respond.

PREPARING LESSONS

Each teacher has their own method for preparing lessons, including how far in advance they do so, what influences what they will do next and how they note the learning intentions. Sometimes schools insist on using a template – and this is often also the case when there is an inspection. The template may work for most teachers, or for the inspector, but not necessarily for a neurodivergent teacher who needs to see things documented in a particular way. If you are observing a lesson, discuss with the teacher how they have prepared and how they record what they will do and have done, rather than insisting they do things a specific way.

Nowadays many teachers prepare and teach lessons using digital tools. This has assisted those who may be concerned about remembering information and the order in which they intend to present material. It has allowed them as well to use multimedia formats which provide a more memorable visual or auditory impact on their learners. Digital tools have also been a big support to teachers who are concerned about their spelling or the legibility of their handwriting. During lessons, some teachers invite students who they know are good at spelling to write for them on whiteboards, and openly admit that they need support from their class to check what they have written is correct. This can also encourage students to feel included and recognise that everyone has both strengths and challenges.

We should remember that it can take some neurodivergent teachers longer to prepare lessons. This may be because they need more time to gather resources, reflect on what they have gained from data through their formative testing of learners, or because they want to check for any grammatical or other errors in what they are going to show to students. It is often also because they can conceive multiple ways of organising and arranging subject content, which makes them better prepared for supporting all students' learning. They may create alternative solutions to completing tasks.

ASSESSING AND REPORTING

In the previous chapter, we discussed the central position of assessment in education – and making sure as far as possible that it is valid, reliable and fair. Marking important assessments can provoke considerable anxiety in neurodivergent teachers who are trying their hardest to follow criteria, be consistent and add up scores correctly. Above all in the marking of high-stakes assessments, such as coursework or portfolios, it is sensible to seek training opportunities, to practise and to work with other colleagues for moderation and standardisation. This way, teachers feel less exposed and more able to ask their own questions so that they are less likely to disadvantage students.

A key part of a teacher's role is to give learners feedback on how well they are doing – what is often called assessment for learning. Feedback is an essential aspect of learning to learn, and of metacognition and self-regulation, all of which we explored in **Chapter 8**. Some teachers may struggle to give written feedback on their learners, again because they lack confidence in their spelling or handwriting. They may feel more able to give feedback if they can do so digitally, not only in written form but, as an alternative, in audio or video. Another positive consequence of this may be that the feedback is then more accessible for students as well. Some teachers may find reviewing learner content easier if it is in a format that can be listened to – for example, by using a text-to-speech application on a digital device.

TEACHERS TALKING TO FAMILIES

Neurodivergent and neurotypical teachers will usually need to communicate with parents. Parents, like some students and teachers, may also be neurodivergent. It is useful to consider how communication can be as effective as possible and not result in miscommunication.

There are three main things to consider here:

1. the means of communication and the extent to which this is comfortable and suitable for all parties – for example, is it by phone, in person, or online?
2. how well prepared a teacher is – whether they are neurodivergent or not – to talk with a family about their child's diagnosed or undiagnosed neurodivergent traits or condition;
3. whether the family members with whom you are communicating are themselves neurodivergent – and may or may not be aware of this.

To repeat Gallwey's formula once more, regarding the first and second considerations, we need to do what we can as teachers to reduce interference in the messages we are giving so that they are delivered and received clearly. Some teachers and family members may not be good at using a particular means of communication and may even be very anxious in the setting of a typical parents' evening. What adjustments could your place of work reasonably make so that those attending don't feel at a disadvantage but are, on the contrary, made to feel welcome and comfortable? Could you ensure feedback or discussions happen in a quieter setting? Could you reinforce what has been said by providing brief written notes as well?

The third consideration above is something which we all need to learn more about as more people understand the potential for differences in the way we process information and communicate. It is hard to be ready for all eventualities when communicating with people you haven't met but if you know individuals will need additional support, you should try to accommodate this. If you meet a family member who you think is neurodivergent but doesn't know it, it is not really your position to suggest they seek this out.

Some parents may be relieved if they discover that they too are displaying similar traits to their child and that they have a recognised condition. Others, though, may still consider this something to hide and even be angry at the suggestion.

You may meet parents who don't like their child being in a class with other neurodivergent students because they consider them disruptive or that they get disproportionate attention. Rather than getting into an argument about this, it may be wiser for a school to take the initiative and offer information about or open opportunities to discuss neurodiversity in education and how being more inclusive benefits everyone in society. Some schools are running neurodiversity campaigns such as those that have been run with the ADHD Foundation in the UK where there are umbrellas displayed in school alongside interactive materials to aid awareness. Increasingly, there are annual neurodiversity awareness campaigns that provide opportunities where information can be shared with students, teachers and parents.

POLICIES AND PROFESSIONAL DEVELOPMENT

Most education workplaces have policies on aspects of life ranging from safeguarding to behaviour, and in relation to equality. There may also be guidance on wellbeing, nutrition and dress code. It is less common to see documentation about neurodiversity and how both students and teachers are supported in their daily lives or can seek redress if they are bullied or victims of micro-aggressions because they are different or request adjustments. Is there a neurodiversity policy where you work?

Make professional development a central part of your workplace and include courses and resources about neurodiversity. This is particularly important for those who are line managers and may have specific expectations of staff that can't always be met by neurodivergent teachers. We explored above how essential it is to get recruitment and onboarding right, but the efforts shouldn't stop there – most individuals would value ongoing, regularly scheduled chats about how they are getting on and what they could do to improve.

You may want to explore coaching as an aspect of professional development, for all teachers and especially for those in positions of responsibility. Coaching, as we described in **Chapter 8**, is a means of facilitating thinking whereby those being coached discover more about themselves and how they could transform their ways of thinking and working, rather than being told what to do and to do it in a certain way. Coaching can help all those who are receptive to it to find and explore new ways of acting, of coping, or of moving on in their careers, and can help individuals see what is getting in the way of them reaching their potential.

Remember as well, as we have said throughout this book, that the exploration and use of inclusive approaches is beneficial for *all* of us, not just those who are neurodivergent. Also, many of the strategies we have described for specific areas of learning or work can be transferred or adapted to other areas. For example, think about your audience and the clarity of your message when you communicate in all formats and circumstances, not just in meetings or inductions. Give staff the opportunity as well to be engaged in discussions and decisions about how they can be the best versions of themselves by reflecting together on barriers and interferences to potential.

NEXT STEPS

Throughout this book we have explored what neurodiversity means in the context of education, what we can do to recognise and celebrate neurodiversity and how we can change the narrative so that we all think about what people *can* do rather than what they cannot.

We have reflected on the barriers erected by society and traditional forms of teaching, learning and assessment that could be reduced, removed or rethought to give as many people as possible the opportunity to participate and succeed.

We know that how we perform personally and professionally is as a result of our genes, our culture and our environments. We know that our situations can change over time and as a result of our interactions with what is around us and with other people. We all have spiky profiles, we all behave variously according to context, and there is no single pathway through education or life.

We hope that we have given you a lot of food for thought that you can use where you live and work. We would like to recommend that you seek further opportunities to learn about neurodiversity, developing yourself by taking courses or reading more on the topic and by listening to and communicating with people around you.

Above all, rather than focusing on difference, focus on *similarity*. We live in a world that benefits enormously from our collective neurodiversity. As we grapple with new and emerging global challenges, our success at a societal level will be defined by our ability to think differently; our ability to thrive will be dependent on harnessing cognitive diversity. Once again, think more about what we can *all* do rather than what some people cannot. In and beyond education, we can call this our 'neurodivers*ability*'.

KEY TAKEAWAYS

- It is hard to estimate how many neurodivergent individuals work in education but based on data about the general population it must be a significant number.
- Little research has been undertaken into the benefits and challenges of being a neurodivergent teacher, but we can make assumptions from what we know about young people and how they react to certain environments and situations.
- More could be done to attract neurodivergent people to the education profession and to support them through recruitment, onboarding and full participation in the complex life of an education workplace.
- We should consider policies, guidelines, opportunities for professional development and our communications with families regarding neurodiversity.
- Much of what we have discussed throughout this book applies to both young people and adults.
- We hope that what you have read and learnt will encourage you to focus on the strengths of neurodiversity, its significance in our lives, what we can do to help others feel the same way and the positive actions we can take to make the most of who we all are.

GLOSSARY

Access arrangements Guidance to schools about exam conditions, and what adjustments can be made for students who need additional support.

Accessible Access to education is often hindered by the presence of barriers which can undermine the individual's opportunities to reach or obtain certain outcomes or goals. These can be experienced in the form of both physical barriers and attitudinal barriers.

Acquired condition A condition that is acquired during an individual's lifetime through trauma, gaining a medical condition, or environmental exposure.

Adaptation The way in which a task, environment or process has been changed to become more accessible.

Allostatic load A term for the cumulative effect of stress and your body's response to stress over time.

Analysis paralysis Where someone feels unable to decide or commit to a single course of action because they find it harder to choose where to start or see too many possibilities and too many links.

Attention deficit hyperactivity disorder (ADHD) A range of behaviours that mean the person has an ability to hyperfocus on areas of interest, may make connections that others don't always notice, have novel ideas and be prepared to try new challenges. They may also find planning and organisation more challenging, which may make it harder to get started with some routine tasks.

Autism spectrum condition (ASC) ASC is often associated with an individual having specific interests and sensory preferences. It can impact communicating effectively with others. The individual may find times of change more stressful.

Barrier   Something that gets in the way of optimising talents, participation, accessing support and/or limits progress.

Belonging   A feeling of being happy, safe or comfortable as part of a particular group – for example, within the family, in a class at school, with work colleagues. This may be as a result of mutual respect and recognition of similarities and differences within the group.

Biopsychosocial model   A model used to consider the biological, psychological and social aspects of an individual.

Cognitive   To do with thinking or conscious mental processes.

Command words   Directive words used with specific meanings on question papers in assessments.

Desirable skills   Skills listed in a job advertisement that a prospective employer considers as being useful but not essential.

Developmental coordination disorder (DCD)   A common developmental condition affecting an individual's motor skills that also has an impact on that person's day-to-day functioning in home, educational and work settings.

Developmental disorder   A condition someone is born with, rather than acquired later in life.

Developmental language disorder (DLD)   A common developmental condition with challenges associated with understanding, processing and using spoken and written language.

Diversity   Describes our wide range of human differences – for example, physical traits, gender, race, class. In the context of this book, we emphasise *cognitive* diversity in recognition of the fact that we all think, learn and behave in a variety of ways.

Down's syndrome   A genetic condition resulting from when someone has a full or partial extra copy of chromosome 21.

Dual coding   Using different types of stimuli to help learners encode information in their brains more effectively – for example, using pictures and words together to aid understanding.

Dyscalculia   Challenges related to the conceptual understanding and use of numbers.

Dyslexia   Challenges relating to the learning and decoding of skills for reading, writing and spelling.

Dyspraxia (see **Developmental coordination disorder**)   A term often used interchangeably with DCD.

Ecological systems model   A model that considers the role that the wider environment of the student plays in shaping their past and present and their ability to access and be included in education.

Ecosystem   The environment (people and place) that someone is placed in and how they interact with this.

Equality   The right of different groups of people to have similar status, rights and opportunities and receive the same treatment.

Equity   The situation in which everyone is treated according to their specific needs rather than being treated equally in the same way as other groups.

fMRI scan   Functional magnetic resonance imaging to evaluate blood flow in the brain and thus see which parts are activated by certain stimuli.

Foetal alcohol spectrum disorder (FASD)   A condition presenting with a specific pattern of mental and physical challenges in a child because of their mother's consumption of alcohol during pregnancy.

Formative assessment   A method used in education through which feedback is given to students to help them improve their learning and simultaneously to teachers to help them improve their ways of teaching.

Hypothalamic–pituitary–adrenal (HPA) axis   The interaction between the hypothalamus, pituitary gland and adrenal glands, which plays a key role in the body's response to stress.

Inclusion   The practices or policy of providing equal access to opportunities and resources for people who might otherwise be excluded or marginalised, such as neurominority groups.

Inclusivity   Creating the right environmental conditions in which all students are valued, respected and can thrive, regardless of their differences.

Interference   A barrier that prevents you from doing something as well as you could do.

International Classification of Functioning, Disability and Health (ICF)   A framework promoted by the WHO for measuring health and disability at both individual and population levels.

LAMIC   Low- and middle-income countries.

Medical model   A way of looking at an individual's problems that places an emphasis on the 'deficit' within an individual, often leading to corrective interventions. Contrast with **Social model** below.

Metacognition   When we *plan*, *monitor* and *evaluate*, and make changes to our own learning behaviours – often also referred to as 'thinking about thinking'.

Micro-metacognition   A technique that enables students to be more conscious of their own learning choices at a more refined level and helps them move towards being reflective.

Mindset   An individual's way of thinking, and their opinions.

Minimal brain dysfunction (MBD)   Term used in the past relating to someone with 'normal' intelligence but with varying combinations of perception, language, attention, impulse control and motor control challenges.

NEET   Not in education, employment or training.

Neurodivergent   Having or related to a type of brain that is often considered as different from a socially constructed or defined norm.

Neurodiversity   The different ways that we all think, move, hear, see, understand, process information and communicate with each other. We are all neurodiverse.

Neurominority   A distinct group or groups of people who diverge from a social norm.

Neurotypical   The group that thinks, moves, hears, sees, understands and processes information which meets social and cultural norms.

Patterns beyond labels   A model that encourages us to look at patterns of challenge or barriers to learning which exist across a group of learners with reference to physical, cognitive and cultural barriers.

Quality First Teaching   A model used in the UK for the delivery of education according to three waves describing students who have (1) no specific needs, (2) additional needs, or (3) more complex needs.

SEMH   Social emotional and mental health.

Social model   A way of looking at an individual's problems, not as 'deficits' or 'disorders' but by the disabling barriers or interferences presented by society. Contrast with **Medical model** above.

Special educational needs   A child has special educational needs if they have a learning problem or disability that makes it more challenging for them to learn via the often prescribed or standardised methods of teaching.

Spectrum   A range of different positions between two extreme points.

Spiky profile   A profile that demonstrates the specific pattern of strengths, challenges and differences across a range of cognitive domains.

Summative assessment   A means of evaluating student learning at the end of an instructional unit by comparing it against a standard or benchmark.

Synaptogenesis   The creation of brain cells and the links between them, and their eventual 'pruning' to strengthen and remove connections according to how much they are used or how useful they are in our lives.

Taxonomy   A classification system for naming and organising things into groups that share similar qualities.

Trait   A characteristic that can produce a particular type of behaviour.

Traumatic brain injury (TBI)   A disruption to brain functioning caused by a sudden and/or violent blow to the head.

Twice exceptional (or **2e**)   Gifted students who also have some form of challenge with engaging with learning or may have a specific disability.

UNESCO   The United Nations Educational, Scientific and Cultural Organization.

Universal design   A means of designing and shaping an environment so as many people as possible can access, participate and make progress, regardless of their age, size, cognitive or physical abilities.

WEIRD   Western, educated, industrialised, rich and democratic countries.

WHO   World Health Organization.

REFERENCES AND FURTHER READING

INTRODUCTION

Gallwey, W.T. (1974–) *The Inner Game series*. https://theinnergame.com/inner-game-books/

UNESCO (2020) *Inclusion in Education: All Means All*. https://en.unesco.org/gem-report/report/2020/inclusion

CHAPTER 1

Blume, H. (1998) Neurodiversity: On the neurological underpinnings of geekdom. *The Atlantic*. https://www.theatlantic.com/magazine/archive/1998/09/neurodiversity/305909/

HM Government (UK) (2009) *Autism Act*. https://www.legislation.gov.uk/ukpga/2009/15/contents

Kirby, A. (2022) *Neurodiversity: Let's Embrace Our Spiky Profiles*. Do-IT Profiler. https://www.linkedin.com/pulse/neurodiversity-lets-embrace-our-spiky-profiles-prof-amanda-kirby/

National Institute of Neurological Disorders and Stroke (NINDS) (2022) *Brain Basics: The Life and Death of a Neuron*. https://www.ninds.nih.gov/health-information/patient-caregiver-education/brain-basics-life-and-death-neuron

Rose, T. (2022) *Collective Illusions: Conformity, Complicity, and the Science of Why We Make Bad Decisions*. Paris: Hachette Go.

Singer, J. (n.d.) *What is Neurodiversity?* https://neurodiversity2.blogspot.com/p/what.html

CHAPTER 2

Boshes, B. and Myklebust, H.R. (1964) A neurological and behavioral study of children with learning disorders. *Neurology, 14,* 7–12. doi: 10.1212/WNL.14.1.7

Bronfenbrenner, U. (2009) *The Ecology of Human Development: Experiments by Nature and Design.* Cambridge, MA: Harvard University Press.

Gillberg, C. (2003) Deficits in attention, motor control, and perception: A brief review. *Archives of Disease in Childhood, 88,* 904–910.

Gillberg, C. (2010) The ESSENCE in child psychiatry: Early symptomatic syndromes eliciting neurodevelopmental clinical examinations. *Research in Developmental Disabilities, 31*(6), 1543–1551. doi: 10.1016/j.ridd.2010.06.002. Epub 2010 Jul 14. PMID: 20634041

Gillberg, C., Fernell, E. and Minnis, H. (2014) Early symptomatic syndromes eliciting neurodevelopmental clinical examinations. *Scientific World Journal,* 710570. https://doi.org/10.1155/2013/710570

Ministerio de Educación y Ciencia de España (1994) *The Salamanca Statement and Framework for Action on Special Needs Education.* Presented at the World Conference on Special Education: Access and Quality. UNESCO. https://unesdoc.unesco.org/ark:/48223/pf0000098427

Oliver, M. (1990) *The Individual and Social Models of Disability.* https://disability-studies.leeds.ac.uk/wp-content/uploads/sites/40/library/Oliver-in-soc-dis.pdf

UNESCO (2000) *Education for all: Meeting our collective commitments.* World Education Forum, Dakar. April. UNESCO.

UNESCO (2006) *Convention against Discrimination in Education (1960) and Articles 13 and 14 (Right to Education) of the International Covenant on Economic, Social and Cultural Rights: A Comparative Analysis.* UNESCO. https://unesdoc.unesco.org/ark:/48223/pf0000145922

UNESCO (2015) *SDG4-Education 2030, Incheon Declaration (ID) and Framework for Action. For the Implementation of Sustainable Development Goal 4, Ensure Inclusive and Equitable Quality Education and Promote Lifelong Learning Opportunities for All,* ED-2016/WS/28. http://uis.unesco.org/sites/default/files/documents/education-2030-incheon-framework-for-action-implementation-of-sdg4-2016-en_2.pdf

United Nations (2015) *Sustainable Development Goal 4 on Education.* United Nations. https://sdgs.un.org/goals/goal4

United States Government (2019) Individuals with Disabilities Education Act (IDEA). https://sites.ed.gov/idea/statute-chapter-33/subchapter-i/1401/30

Warnock, M. (1978) *Special Educational Needs: Report of the Committee of Enquiry into the Education of Handicapped Children and Young People.* HMSO. http://www.educationengland.org.uk/documents/warnock/warnock1978.html

Warnock, M. (1979) Children with special needs: The Warnock Report. *British Medical Journal, 1,* 667–668.

CHAPTER 3

Chang, H.-K., Hsu, J.-W., Wu, J.-C., Huang., K.-L., Chang, H.-C., Bai, Y.-M., Chen, T.-J. and Chen, M.-H. (2018) Traumatic brain injury in early childhood and risk of attention deficit/hyperactivity disorder and autism spectrum disorder: A nationwide longitudinal study. *Journal of Clinical Psychiatry, 79*(6). doi: 10.4088/JCP.17m11857

Chitsabesan, P., Lennox, C., Williams, H., Tariq, O. and Shaw, J. (2015) Traumatic brain injury in juvenile offenders: Findings from the comprehensive health assessment tool study and the development of a specialist linkworker service. *Journal of Head Trauma Rehabilitation, 30,* pp. 106–115.

Huw Williams, W. and Chitsabesan, P. (2016) *Young People with Traumatic Brain Injury in Custody.* Barrow Cadbury Trust. https://barrowcadbury. org.uk/wp-content/uploads/2016/07/Disability_Trust_linkworker_2016-Lores.pdf

Kent, H. and Williams, H. (2021) *Traumatic Brain Injury.* Her Majesty's Inspectorate of Probation. https://www.justiceinspectorates.gov.uk/hmiprobation/wp-content/uploads/sites/5/2021/08/Academic-Insights-Kent-and-Williams-LL-v2.0-RMdocx.pdf

Kirby, A. (2022) *Balls in the Buckets.* Do-IT Profiler. https://doitprofiler.com/insight/wrong-coloured-balls-neurodiversity-diagnosis/

Moldavsky, M., Pass, S. and Sayal, K. (2014) Primary school teachers' attitudes about children with attention deficit/hyperactivity disorder and the role of pharmacological treatment. *Clinical Child Psychology and Psychiatry*, *19*(2), 202–216. doi: 10.1177/1359104513485083

Sariaslan, A., Sharp, D.J., D'Onofrio, B.M., Larsson, H. and Fazel, S. (2016) Long-term outcomes associated with traumatic brain injury in childhood and adolescence: A nationwide Swedish cohort study of a wide range of medical and social outcomes. *PLoS Med*, *23*, *13*(8), e1002103. doi: 10.1371/journal.pmed.1002103. PMID: 27552147; PMCID: PMC4995002

CHAPTER 4

Beck, A.E. (1994) On universities: J. Tuzo Wilson Medal acceptance speech. *Elements: Newsletter of the Canadian Geophysical Union*, *12*, 7–9.

Benton, T., Boyd, R. and Njoroge, W. (2021) Addressing the global crisis of child and adolescent mental health. *Journal of the American Medical Association*, *175*(11), 1108–1110.

Blakemore, S.J. and Frith, U. (2005) *The Learning Brain*. Hoboken, NJ: Blackwell.

Burnett, D. (2021) *Psycho-Logical*. London: Guardian Faber.

Cambridge Assessment International Education (2020) Education Brief: Learner Wellbeing. https://www.cambridgeinternational.org/Images/612684-learner-wellbeing.pdf

Deci, E.L. and Ryan, R.M. (2000) The 'what' and 'why' of goal pursuits: Human needs and the self-determination of behavior. *Psychological Inquiry*, *11*(4), 227–268.

Dweck, C. (1999) *Self-Theories: Their Role in Motivation, Personality, and Development*. Hove: Psychology Press.

Engel, G. (1979) The biopsychosocial model and the education of health professionals. *General Hospital Psychiatry*, *1*(2), 156–165.

Huppert, F.A. (2009) Psychological well-being: Evidence regarding its causes and consequences. *Applied Psychology: Health and Well-being*, *1*(2), 137–164.

International Baccalaureate (2021) *Supporting Student Wellbeing in A Digital Learning Environment.* https://ibo.org/research/policy-research/supporting-student-wellbeing-in-a-digital-learning-environment-2021/

Kirby, A. and Cleaton, M. (n.d.) *Neurodiversity 101: And Mental Health.* Cardiff: Do-IT Solutions.

Kirby, A. and Cleaton, M. (n.d.) *Neurodiversity 101: Psychosocial Outcomes.* Cardiff: Do-IT Solutions.

Mancini V.O., Rigoli, D., Cairney, J. and Roberts L.D. (2016) The elaborated environmental stress hypothesis as a framework for understanding the association between motor skills and internalizing problems: A mini-review. *Frontiers in Psychology, 7,* 239.

Maslow, A.H. (1943) A theory of human motivation. *Psychological Review, 50*(4), 370–396.

Rose, R., Howley, M., Fergusson, A. and Jament, J. (2009) Mental health and special educational needs: Exploring a complex relationship. *British Journal of Special Education, 36.* doi: 10.1111/j.1467-8578.2008.00409.x

Ryan, R.M. and Deci, E.L. (2000) Self-determination theory and the facilitation of intrinsic motivation, social development, and well-being. *American Psychologist, 55*(1), 68.

World Health Organization (WHO) (2018) *Mental Health: Strengthening Our Response.* https://www.who.int/news-room/fact-sheets/detail/mental-health-strengthening-our-response

CHAPTER 5

American Psychiatric Association (2013) *Diagnostic and Statistical Manual of Mental Disorders* (5th edn). American Psychiatric Association.

Armstrong, T. (2012) *Neurodiversity in the Classroom: Strength-Based Strategies to Help Students with Special Needs Succeed in School and Life.* Alexandra, VA: ASCD.

Bronfenbrenner, U. (2009) *The Ecology of Human Development: Experiments by Nature and Design.* Cambridge, MA: Harvard University Press. ISBN 0-674-22457-4

Collinson, C. (2012) Dyslexics in time machines and alternate realities: Thought experiments on the existence of dyslexics, 'dyslexia' and 'lexism'. *British Journal of Special Education, 39*(2), 63–70.

Gallwey, W.T. (1974–) *The Inner Game series.* https://theinnergame.com/inner-game-books/

Hain, A., Zaghhaui, A.E. and Taylor, C.L. (2018) *Board 164: Promoting Neurodiversity in Engineering through Undergraduate Research Opportunities for Students with ADHD.* Paper presented at 2018 ASEE Annual Conference and Exposition. https://peer.asee.org/29969

Naraian, S. (2019) Precarious, debilitated and ordinary: Rethinking (in) capacity for inclusion. *Curriculum Inquiry, 49*(4), 464–484. doi: 10.1080/03626784.2019.1659100

Neuman, S.B. and Roskos, K. (2005) Whatever happened to developmentally appropriate practice in early literacy? *YC Young Children, 60*(4), 22–26. https://search-proquest-com.ezproxye.bham.ac.uk/docview/197690782?accountid=8630

University of Bath (2018) *ADD/ADHD: Implications for Study in Higher Education.* Bath: University of Bath.

Wing, L. (2003) *The Autistic Spectrum.* London: Robinson.

World Health Organization (WHO) (2001) *International Classification of Functioning, Disability and Health: ICF.* Geneva: World Health Organization. https://apps.who.int/iris/handle/10665/42407.

CHAPTER 6

CAST (2020) *Universal Design for Learning at a Glance and UDL Guidelines.* Wakefield, MA: CAST. http://www.cast.org/impact/universal-design-for-learning-udl

Lebeer, J. (2016) Significance of the Feuerstein approach in neurocognitive rehabilitation. *NeuroRehabilitation, 39*(1). doi: 10.3233/NRE-161335. PMID: 27341359

Montessori Group (2020) *The Montessori Network.* Laren, Netherlands: Montessori Group. https://montessori-group.com/network/

National Geographic (2011) *7 Billion: Are You Typical?* https://www.youtube.com/watch?v=4B2xOvKFFz4

Robinson, K. (2006) *Do Schools Kill Creativity?* TED Conferences. https://www.ted.com/talks/sir_ken_robinson_do_schools_kill_creativity?language=en

Rose, T. (2017) *The End of Average: How to Succeed in a World that Values Sameness.* London: Penguin.

CHAPTER 7

Armstrong, P. (2010) *Bloom's Taxonomy.* Vanderbilt University Center for Teaching. https://cft.vanderbilt.edu/guides-sub-pages/blooms-taxonomy/

Bloom, B.S. (1956) *Taxonomy of Educational Objectives: The Cognitive Domain.* Philadelphia, PA: David McKay.

CAST (2020) *Universal Design for Learning at a Glance and UDL Guidelines.* Wakefield, MA: CAST. http://www.cast.org/impact/universal-design-for-learning-udl

Colley, M. (2006) *Living with Dyspraxia.* London: Jessica Kingsley.

Eaton, R. and Osborne, A. (2019) *Going Beyond the Label: Reframing the Narrative of Disability Support and Inclusive Practice.* Swansea University. SAILS conference.

Osborne, A. (2021) *Inclusive Assessment Strategies.* Bath: University of Bath. https://teachinghub.bath.ac.uk/curriculum-principles/embrace-assessment-for-learning/inclusive-assessment-strategies/

Ross, H. (2017) An exploration of teachers' agency and social relationships within dyslexia-support provision in an English secondary school. *British Journal of Special Education,* 44(2).

Syed, M. (2015) *Black Box Thinking: The Surprising Truth About Success (and Why Some People Never Learn from Their Mistakes).* London: John Murray.

CHAPTER 8

Downey, M. (2014) *Effective Modern Coaching.* London: LID.

Haug, P. (2017) Understanding inclusive education: Ideals and reality. *Scandinavian Journal of Disability Research,* 19(3), 206–217.

Jessop, T. and Tomas, C. (2017) The implications of programme assessment patterns for student learning. *Assessment and Evaluation in Higher Education*, 42(6), 990–999. doi: 10.1080/02602938.2016.1217501

Osborne, A., Angus-Cole, K. and Venables, L. (forthcoming, 2023) *From Wellbeing to Welldoing*. London: Sage.

Paivio, A. (1971) *Imagery and Verbal Processes*. New York: Holt, Rinehart & Winston.

Paivio, A. (1986) *Mental Representations: A Dual-Coding Approach*. New York: Oxford University Press.

Perkins, D. (1992) *Smart Schools: Better Thinking and Learning for Every Child*. New York: Free Press.

Schön, D.A. (1987) *Educating the Reflective Practitioner: Toward a New Design for Teaching and Learning in the Professions*. Hoboken, NJ: Jossey-Bass.

Whitmore, J. (2017) *Coaching for Performance: The Principles and Practices of Coaching and Leadership*. Boston: Nicholas Brealey.

CHAPTER 9

Child, S. and Ellis, P. (2021) *The What, Why and How of Assessment: A Guide for Teachers and School Leaders*. Thousand Oaks, CA: Corwin.

Duncan, H. and Purcell, C. (2017) Equity or advantage? The effect of receiving access arrangements in university exams on humanities students with specific learning difficulties (SpLD). *Widening Participation and Lifelong Learning*, 19(2). https://doi.org/10.5456/WPLL.19.2.6

Duncan, H. and Purcell, C. (2019) Consensus or contradiction? A review of the current research into the impact of granting extra time in exams to students with specific learning difficulties (SpLD). *Journal of Further and Higher Education*, 44(4), 439–453. https://doi.org/10.1080/0309877X.2019.1578341

Gallwey, W.T. (1974–) *The Inner Game* series. https://theinnergame.com/inner-game-books/

National Center on Educational Outcomes (n.d.) *Universal Design of Assessments*. https://nceo.info/Assessments/universal_design

Putwain, D. (2021) *Testing Times: When Taking (And Not Taking) Assessments Becomes a Source of Anxiety.* Conference keynote. Cambridge Assessment International Education. https://www.cambridgeinternational.org/support-and-training-for-schools/cambridge-schools-conference/previous-conferences/june-2021-online-conference/

Vidal Rodeiro, C.L. (2021) *Equality of Students' Access to Access Arrangements and their Impact on Students' Performance.* Cambridge Assessment Research Report. Cambridge Assessment.

Woods, L. and Ellis, P. (2022) *Top Tips for Supporting Students with Special Educational Needs and Disabilities Before and During Exams.* Cambridge Assessment International Education. https://blog.cambridgeinternational.org/top-tips-for-supporting-students-with-send-before-and-during-exams/

CHAPTER 10

Glazzard, J. and Dale, K. (2015) 'It takes me half a bottle of whisky to get through one of your assignments': Exploring one teacher educator's experiences of dyslexia. *Dyslexia, 21,* 177–192. https://doi.org/10.1002/dys.1493

Jacobs, L., Collyer, E., Lawrence, C. and Glazzard, J. (2021) 'I've got something to tell you. I'm dyslexic': The lived experiences of trainee teachers with dyslexia. *Teaching and Teacher Education, 104.* https://doi.org/10.1016/j.tate.2021.103383

Smith, T. and Kirby, A. (2021) *Neurodiversity at Work: Drive Innovation, Performance and Productivity with a Neurodiverse Workforce.* London: Kogan Page.

Wood, R., Crane, L., Happé, F., Morrison, A. and Moyse, R. (2022) *Learning from Autistic Teachers: How to be a Neurodiversity-Inclusive School.* London: Jessica Kingsley.

INDEX

Page numbers followed by 'f' denote figures. Page numbers followed by 't' denote tables.